Did
Ye Hear
Mammy
Died?

Séamas O'Reilly

Did Ye Hear Mammy Died?

FLEET

2021

FLEET

First published in Great Britain in 2021 by Fleet

3 5 7 9 10 8 6 4

Copyright © Séamas O'Reilly 2021

The moral right of the author has been asserted.

The article on page 199 is reproduced by kind permission of the *Derry Journal*.

A CIP catalogue record for this book
is available from the British Library.

Hardback ISBN 978-0-7088-9922-9
Trade Paperback ISBN 978-0-7088-9924-3

Typeset in Bembo by M Rules
Printed and bound in Great Britain by
Clays Ltd, Elcograf S.p.A.

Papers used by Fleet are from well-managed forests
and other responsible sources.

Fleet
An imprint of
Little, Brown Book Group
Carmelite House
50 Victoria Embankment
London EC4Y 0DZ

An Hachette UK Company
www.hachette.co.uk

www.littlebrown.co.uk

To Daddy.
For Mammy.

Contents

1

Did Ye Hear Mammy Died?

One thing they don't tell you about mammies is that when they die you get new trousers. On my first full day as a half-orphan, I remember fiddling with unfamiliar cords as Margaret held my cheek and told me Mammy was a flower.

She and her husband Phillie were close friends of my parents, and their presence is one of the few memories that survive from that period, most specifically the conversation Margaret had with me there and then. 'Sometimes,' croaked Margaret in a voice bent ragged from two days' crying, 'when God sees a particularly pretty flower, He'll take it up from Earth, and put it in his own garden.' Margaret held me in the sort of tight, worried grip usually reserved for heaving lambs up a ladder. As she clenched my hand and told me God had specially marked my mother for death, a tear-damp thumb traced small circles on my temple. She stroked my hair.

It was nice to think that Mammy was so well-liked by God, since she was a *massive* fan. She went to all his gigs – Mass, prayer groups, marriage guidance meetings; and had all the action figures – small Infant of Prague statuettes, much larger Infant of Prague statuettes, little blue plastic flasks of holy water in the shape of God's own Mammy herself. So, in one sense, Margaret's version of events was kind of comforting. It placed my mother's death in that category of stories where people met their heroes, like Maureen Bouvaird getting a hug from Daniel O'Donnell in the Mount Errigal Hotel. Only Mammy's death was even better, since Mrs Bouvaird didn't get to live outside Daniel's house forever thereafter, however much she would have liked to. As it happens, witnesses said Maureen cried so much she hyperventilated, leaving a shining snail's trail of snot arching from Daniel's jumper to the floor. Thereafter, the sexy eunuch of Irish country music waved her to the medical tent, where she spent the remainder of the evening clutching an icepack to blue curls in glazed, mumbling bliss.

As Margaret reassured me that God was an avaricious gardener intent on murdering my loved ones any time he pleased, I concentrated once more on my new corduroy slacks, summoned from the aether as if issued by whichever government department administers to the needs of all the brave little boys with dead, flowery mams – an infant grief action pack stuffed with trousers, sensible underpants, cod liver oil tablets and a solar-powered calculator.

The cords were new and clean and inordinately delightful to fiddle with, most especially when I flicked my finger up and down their pleasing grooves, stopping only each time a superheated nail forced a change of hands. I think it's fair to say I had no idea what was going on, save that this was all very sad and, worse, making Margaret sad. In that way of five-year-olds, I feared sadness in adults above all things, so I leaned my head upon Margaret's shoulder to reassure her that her words had scrubbed things clean. In truth, I found the flower story unsettling. I couldn't help picturing Mammy – lovely, tired and blue-tinged in her flowy white hospital gown – awakening to a frenzy of mechanical beeping as the roof caved in and tubes burst from machines.

'God takes the most beautiful ones for himself,' she repeated in a tired rasp, as I envisaged the room pelted from above by ceiling plaster, maybe an oncologist or two getting knocked out by falling smoke alarms, God's two great probing fingers smashing through the roof to relocate Mammy to that odd garden he kept in heaven, presumably so he'd have something to do on Sundays.

In fact, my mother died from the breast cancer that had spun a cruel, mocking thread through her life for four years. The hospital rang my father at 3 a.m. on Thursday 17 October 1991. Their exact words went unrecorded, but the general gist was that he'd want to get there quick. I can't imagine the horror of that morning, my father racing dawn, chain-smoking as he managed the ninety-minute drive from Derry to Belfast in less than an hour. When he arrived, she had already passed. Sheila O'Reilly was dead, and my father drove back to Derry as the sole parent of eleven children.

From certain angles, the circumstances of my upbringing are disarmingly baroque. I agree, for example, that the whole eleven kids thing is a bit much. My parents' remarkable fecundity had long been something of a cause célèbre to friends or, indeed, any random person who could count past ten, or had passed our scraggly-haired forms in the big white minibus in which we drove around. Nicknamed, with some inevitability, the O'Reillymobile, this vehicle cemented our place as an oddity wherever we went, and while I'm not saying everyone we knew mocked us as a gaggle of freaks, I'd find it hard to understand if they didn't.

Passing us on the road during the school run, you would have seen a mildly frazzled man at the wheel, muttering at traffic through a woolly fog of cigar smoke. This man, resplendent in a two-tone suit and with beautifully combed blond hair, is my father, Joe, or *Daddy*, as Northern Irish speech has it. Daddy was, for reasons that will become obvious, the bright, shining star of my childhood, and, quite possibly, human life on Earth during this period. His hypothetical tension behind the wheel on this entirely notional morning might have been the result of one of us forgetting to put on shoes, neglecting to go to the toilet, or ingeniously weaponising a nosebleed against their nearest sibling.

He might have been stressed by that morning's check-point run, the dystopian rigmarole undertaken by everyone who lived on Northern Ireland's border with the Republic of Ireland, during which army patrolmen would have commanded him to present ID as they manoeuvred their long, mirrored stick under the vehicle on the off-chance he'd paused ahead of the school run to place explosive materiel underneath his eleven infants' feet. Of course, you could also just have happened to catch him during the nerve-obliterating period between 1999 and 2001, when no fewer than six of his daughters were simultaneously teenagers. I can't imagine what that was like, and I was there. To be honest, the wonder isn't so much that my father was frazzled, but that he managed to avoid going flamboyantly insane.

Contrary to the expectations of non-Irish people, it was highly unusual to have a family so large. Among my parents' generation, it might have been slightly more common, particularly in rural communities, but by the eighties and nineties, such tallies were vanishingly rare. My parents were formidably – perhaps recklessly – Catholic, but even among the ranks of the devout, families with five kids were seldom seen. Seven would have been considered crisply eccentric, and nine plainly mad. To be one of eleven was singularly, fizzily demented. At best, you were the child of sex maniacs; at worst, the creepy scions of some bearded recluse amassing weapons in the hills. It didn't help that we were so close in age and travelled, often singing, in the kind of large, vaguely municipal transport vehicle usually reserved for separatist church groups and volleyball teams made up of young offenders.

In some school years, it was easier to isolate the age groups in which we did not have a representative. In primary school we once had emissaries in six out of seven classes. We've since been told tales of completely unconnected third parties working out their relative age groups by referring to which O'Reilly was in their year. Even within our own home, it was necessary to erect internal subdivisions that simplified things. This we did by separating into three distinct castes, which ran in age order thus: the Big Ones (Sinead, Dara and Shane), the Middle Ones (Maeve, Orla, Mairead and Dearbhaile) and the Wee Ones (Caoimhe, me, Fionnuala and Conall). When my mother died, the youngest of us was two. I was myself three weeks shy of my sixth birthday; the celebration of that was, I have been led to believe, a decidedly subdued affair.

It's an infuriating quirk of the brain that I remember my first taste of a banana sandwich but not the moment I was told Mammy had died. The closest I can manage must be some moments – perhaps hours – later: a clear image of walking through pyjama-clad siblings who were crying in all directions. It was morning, but since Daddy had left so early the curtains hadn't yet been thrown open, a practice fastidiously encouraged the second he woke. This tinged everything with a dark, greyish unfamiliarity that only added to the queasy gloom of the moment.

There are differing accounts of how the news was delivered, but we know Daddy rang to tell us some time after 6 a.m. Some remember Sinead answering the phone, others her pleading with Dara to get it. The Big Ones – then aged thirteen, fifteen and seventeen respectively – had understood the gravity of those last few trips to the hospital better than the rest of us. To children reared to believe no news was good news, a 6 a.m. phone call bore all the gut-punching potentiality of, well, *news*.

We'd been to see Mammy the preceding weekend. I once more find I only have very faint memories of that final visit. I can see her in bed, tired and pale, laughing through the web of tubes taped to her face like a child's art project, but it's impossible to know if this was on that occasion or some earlier trip. Those tubes were a common point of reference for us in the years after her death, my sister Maeve becoming convinced they'd strangled her. By contrast, I have quite floridly detailed memories from later on that day, playing outside in the tall trees that lined the clinic, presumably after the Wee Ones had been removed to give my parents some space from their more oblivious children.

Apart from that I can remember very little of that week, save that morning on the couch with Margaret and a smattering of sensations from the subsequent wake. My father had called Phillie and Margaret with the news before he left Belfast, so they could come over to our house and look in on us until he returned. They arrived in the early morning to a surreal mess of sobbing. It also fell to them to intercept Anne as she pulled in to begin her day's work, around seven. Anne was a saintly woman who tended to the house and its numerous infant contents, most especially since Mammy had fallen ill. Anne was particularly beloved of my mother for her superhuman propensity for calm, an invaluable asset on those days when the cruel humiliations of cancer seemed inexplicable, or she simply found herself without the will to talk.

Anne was as steady as rain and implacable as taxes; the kind of strong, rooted Donegal woman you could imagine blithely tutting if her hair caught fire. Looking out the kitchen window past our own shaken tears, we watched as the news made even her steadfast frame crumple backward. We saw her face collapse and her knees buckle, hands grasping her mouth before they steadied themselves on the car door behind.

This was, of course, a mere precursor to the sight of my father returning to sobs and screams, holding us all as we heaved, and crying loudly himself. The sight of my father crying was so dizzyingly perverse that I couldn't have been more shocked and appalled if bats had flown out of his mouth. Daddy's stoicism was as solid a fixture in my life as rain, or Savlon. This was the man who had forged time and space with his own rough hands, unafraid of heights or the dark or spiders or anything, save for being caught without some WD-40 when he needed it. In many ways, my father's grief hit me harder than anything else. It would be from the wreckage of this moment that he would reassemble the universe for us.

Mammy's body returned that afternoon, and was to be waked in our home. While the house was filling up, me and the other Wee Ones were being kept out of the way as things were made ready. I was mesmerised by the strange acoustic novelties now occurring in rooms removed of their furniture; the echoing clang of chairs and tables dragged about the place; the strange, loud, reverberating clicks of clocks that went, despite tradition, unstopped. It was customary for mirrors to be covered too, but Daddy had forgone both these measures since, for all his religious devotion, he saw them as affectation.

Our great big bungalow lay on the border of Derry and Donegal, with 'on the border' being here quite literal. Where our fence ended, so did the international jurisdictions of the United Kingdom of Great Britain and Northern Ireland, its Crown Dependencies, all British Overseas Territories and the wider Commonwealth. Situated as far out from the city as it was, we rarely had many visitors, let alone enough to crowd our decidedly roomy environs. Now, there were people everywhere. Moreover, there was a sense that these were all people I'd simply never seen in our house before. They weren't strangers exactly, they just weren't *house* friends. These were people I'd only ever seen in the middle of town; ones who'd stop Mammy with a holler and a hooting laugh, as if bumping into someone in a shop was the greatest miracle since that pig in Ballinasloe that sang hymns. They'd grab her arm and talk a few feet above me, invariably bending down to smush my face and ask, 'Dear God, Sheila, which one's this now?' They'd never guess my name, since I was on the younger end, and it was generally hard enough for my parents to keep track, but I was pinched and cuddled and told I was the spit of whichever sibling it was that they did happen to know. And now here they were, in our kitchen, the life squashed out of them, all serious and nervy as they carried dishes about the place and sheepishly searched, cupboard by cupboard, for whisks or dish cloths. Over these two days we would host a throng of well-wishers who'd come to pay their respects, see how we were doing, and inevitably bring us food, plates or cutlery. There were casseroles and tureens of soup and pyramids of vol-au-vents being shaped and reshaped like ice sculptures as they sat on that huge kitchen table, which had been moved especially for the purpose. This may have been the single biggest change; the table's twelve-foot length completely altering the room's dimensions when placed against the opposite wall, under that giant, high, ugly mirror, in which I was still many years from catching my own reflection.

In the time-honoured tradition of all Irish crises, sandwiches were liberally distributed. Egg and onion, of course, but also ham, and not merely the thin, wet slices you got for school lunches, but the thick, rough-cut chunks that still had the fat on – the type used exclusively by millionaires, Vikings and, it was taken for granted, Protestants. To add to the general sense of occasion, fifteen-year-old Dara had been dispatched to Lapsley's to pick up two hundred Regal King Size cigarettes.

The 160 that made it back from the shop were distributed around the house on oblong trays of polished silver, the kind of dish more typically reserved for bringing meat joints to neighbours' houses. Individual cigarettes were also offered freely to guests by hand, as if we were not a gathering of grief-stricken Northern Irish Catholics at all, but a cabal of New York sophisticates toasting a dazzling new biography of Lyndon Johnson.

Still more people filed in. Friends my mother had accumulated in her six short years teaching in Derry, but whom her children knew only by titled rank, like Mr O'Mahoney, Father Collins, Sister Deirdre, Dr Cleary. And more cups, plates, cutlery, napkins, sandwiches, not to mention all manner of glazed meats and boiled vegetables, wrapped in foil and on plates their donors were prepared to never see again. The sheer mass of food on display may have given an outsider the impression that we were doubly afflicted; not merely a giant family bereft of a loving mother, but one just pulled from six weeks under an avalanche, in which they'd had little or no access to potato salads, gravy or fruitcakes in that time.

I'm not sure if this was the origin of our family's long-standing collection of dark, dense fruitcakes, but I've always believed it to be the case. The notion that anyone enjoys Irish fruitcake – a foodstuff that boasts the consistency, shine and taste of a wet boxing glove – is so fanciful I've long theorised that every gifting of a fruitcake is just that person offloading one they themselves were cruelly gifted some days (or years) earlier. Brown, thick and studded with dried fruits of dubious age and origin, fruitcakes are the nutritional equivalent of concussion. They are so unpalatable, so repulsive, so reminiscent of a bundled-up tarpaulin that's spent a week in the rain, you'd have little chance of getting someone to accept one unless the occasion precluded their making a scene. I'm still largely convinced that all of rural Ireland is engaged in a dense, berried pyramid scheme devoted to circulating the same thousand cakes in a never-ending merry-go-round of spongy offal. Despite our best efforts at redistribution, there were fruitcakes in our house that stayed for years. Some of them we dared not move for fear they'd become load bearing.

In a kindly gesture, Phillie Riordan had brought dozens of spirit miniatures, the little overpriced booze bottles you get in a hotel minibar. These were sincerely appreciated, not least by Dara, who instituted another light tax for his own ends before decamping to the garage to play pool for the evening. Phillie had no doubt procured the miniatures via respectable means, but the odd specificity of such an offering delighted those for whom it conjured images of our upright and respectable GP pilfering his haul from hotel minibars over several years. There were also the kind of large, stainless-steel caterer's teapots you see at church fairs. Did we borrow those too from the convent, like we did the dozens of sandy-coloured folding wooden chairs? The latter now stretched from the back door and through the kitchen, out the front hall, and up against the piano in the dining room where Mammy lay in her coffin, on a table that was too high for me to see her without being lifted.

With its folded chairs, industrial quantities of tea and expanding population of desolate mourners, the house soon took on the appearance of a field hospital. Beside those standing in twos and threes, engaging in murmured conversation, still more slumped alone in chairs, rendered insensible to others by stifled sobs. Everywhere stood puffy-eyed people with features so red and blotchy it was as if bandages had just been ripped off their faces. I can still remember the slowly disappearing mirage of finger-shaped, blood-evacuated flesh on Giovanni Doran's cheeks as he withdrew the hand that clasped his face so he could shake my father's.

There were, everywhere, people who'd been jarringly removed from their appropriate contexts. Mr O'Mahoney, who commanded the dignity of a sphinx in the secondary school I would later attend, was reduced to fumbling his way through a chat with my older brother Shane, in which he told his then-thirteen-year-old student that his own mother had recently died, and thus he knew what Shane was going through. A polite type, Shane was nevertheless incapable of hiding his contempt for the equivalence. Thereafter, the conversation took on that stilted air common to those chats you have with sales staff once they tell you the price of an item and you keep talking only so they'll never suspect you don't regularly spend £28 on lemon-scented handwash.

Most guests, already sombre and teary when they arrived, were stunned into traumatic shock once they greeted the body. Gripping the coffin's edge, they stared in dejection at my mother, who lay stately, pale and dead at forty-three. Some regarded her casket as if it were a grisly wound they'd discovered on their own body, registering the sight with a loud gasping horror that made all around them redouble their own racking sobs. Some witnesses collapsed in the manner of someone cruelly betrayed, as if they'd arrived at the whole maudlin affair on the understanding they were being driven to a Zumba class.

In any case, a sniffled consensus prevailed that my mother

looked 'just like herself'. This sentiment was always spoken with an air of relief that suggested Irish morticians were sometimes in the habit of altering the appearance of the dead for a laugh, but on this occasion had read the generally melancholy feeling in the room and realised it would be best to make up her face to look as much as possible as it had in life. In a nice touch, you might have noted, her clothes had also been chosen from her own wardrobe, rather than from some jolly old hamper in the corner of the morgue filled with feather boas, pirate hooks and floppy, felt-lined cowboy hats. Many's the wake, you might presume, owed its lively atmosphere to the hilarious sight of your late Auntie Pauline dressed head to toe as Henry VIII.

And so this cycle repeated; people arriving bearing fruitcake, ashen-faced, clasping hands and embracing those of us there gathered, only to see the body and suffer an emotional collapse that might range anywhere from throttled gasp to guttural wailing. Hundreds would come in the next two days, causing hushed embarrassment among those who inadvertently arrived when things were already hectic, or had realised they'd called at a more prominent time than their relation to the deceased might warrant. As always, even in kindest company, an unspoken hierarchy of grief asserted itself.

Wakes surround you, smother you even, with loved ones and acquaintances and workmates and long-lost pals, prompting a cycle of social interaction that gives the entire process a strangely unreal tinge. Perhaps that's the point, and the whole system is just a ruse aimed at preventing emotional breakdown by demanding a ritual period of event management for the mourner. Of course you can be alone with your dark, broiling thoughts, but only once you've made and distributed six hundred cups of tea.

My memories are scattered: Dara and Shane playing pool in the garage, and the latter winning since the former was getting increasingly merry on pilfered spirits; the twins, Orla and Maeve, acting adult and serene, though they were not yet twelve; my youngest brother, Conall, six weeks from turning three years old, looking even more confused than I did, being passed from person to person in a daisy chain of cuddles so never-ending I don't know that his feet touched the ground all day. My own contribution to people's memories of the wake is somewhat less dignified than I'd like, but has become a venerable classic on those boozy nights when my family come together and retell our favourite mortifying tales about ourselves.

A system had been put in place to try to marshal the movements of us Wee Ones, who were a bit too young and, let's face it, thick to understand precisely what was going on. Hence my being fussed over with sadness by Margaret, or Anne, or any of the Big or Middle Ones. Of course, they couldn't repress my ebullient run-around ways for ever, and before long, I was wandering free through the gathered mourners. I was simply too young to grasp that the only thing sadder than a five-year-old crying because his mammy has died is a five-year-old wandering around with a smile on his face because he hasn't yet understood what that means. We laugh about it now, but it really is hard for me to imagine the effect I must have had, skipping sunnily through the throng, appalling each person upon their entry to the room by thrusting my beaming, three-foot frame in front of them like a chipper little maître d', with the cheerful enquiry:

'Did ye hear Mammy died?'

Did Ye Hear Mammy Died?

I don't remember faces dropping, nor anguished sighs, but I'm told I accumulated many such reactions before someone came up and stopped me from traumatising any more of these good people. The solemnity, not to mention the permanence, of my mother's death was lost on me then, and it would take a while to sell it in a way I really took to heart. Months later, in much the same manner of a man who remembers a packet of Rolos in his coat pocket, I'd straighten my back with delight and perkily ask the nearest larger person when Mammy was coming back, on account of how she'd been dead for ages and was, surely by now, overdue a return.

The funeral itself was a beautiful affair, with eight priests scattered from chancel to apse in Long Tower church. The service was led by Bishop Edward Daly, a man made famous by his fearless work on Bloody Sunday, traversing the Bogside with his blood-stained handkerchief. He was a family friend back in my dad's home town, a man who'd been babysat by my granny in his youth. When my parents moved to Derry, he drove them about and showed them what was what. Just six years later, he was officiating at Mammy's funeral. There were over a thousand attendees, and other than standard weeping, the silence was broken only by the softly warped lilt of Long Tower's great organ and Dearbhaile, three years my senior, who screamed so hard her shoe fell off, and Phillie had to take her outside to be sedated.

Mammy was laid to rest in Brandywell cemetery, high up the steep, grassy hill that runs up into Creggan, looking down over Brandywell Road and Derry City's stadium. Some years later, a fibreglass statue of a paramilitary volunteer was erected a few

15

graves in front of hers, a fascinating departure from the ambience of angels and urns graveyards typically aim for. Mounted by the INLA – very much the Andrew Ridgeley of Irish republicanism – it was a striking addition to the neighbourhood. The aims and deeds of the INLA are too complex to go into here, but it is odd that, to this day, any time I visit my mother's grave it hovers on the edge of my vision like a giant G.I. Joe, only one who's about to give a prepared warning to the world's media. If you were to construct a heavy-handed visual metaphor for how large a shadow the Troubles cast over everything in Northern Ireland during my childhood, it wouldn't be a bad shout.

On the way home, Daddy rolled down the window of the hearse and thanked the policemen marshalling the traffic at Nixon's Corner. This was the checkpoint that lay two miles from our house, the very same one we'd go through each morning. That they had taken the time to facilitate the cortège and its followers was a bending of protocol that my father greatly appreciated, the kind of touching moment you could imagine Van Morrison singing about, when he wasn't phlegmily screaming at some studio engineer.

In the months that followed, left more and more to ourselves, the shock would subside and the slow, rumbling grief would come in successive, parallel waves. The impacts would come to each of us individually and at different speeds, and then be magnified by all of the subsequent considerations of everyone else's grief, cross-bred and multiplied by the twelve of us trying to make sense of it, whether together or apart. When you lost the energy to be sad, anger would tag in for a relief shift. My older siblings would work through their own grief and then consider the horror that we younger members still had to go through, and the abject desolation of the whole thing would reheat inside them all over again.

My mother wouldn't be there any more to kiss grazed knees or carry me to bed when I pretended to have fallen asleep in the car or dry my hair with the static force of a hydroelectric dam. She would never cock an eyebrow at the socialist-tinged T-shirts or abstruse electronica of my teens. She would never smile politely at girlfriends she found overfamiliar, or text me to say she loved them the second I got home. Mammy would never send a text message full stop. She would never read an email or live to see the words 'website' or 'car boot sale' enter a dictionary. Mammy didn't even live to see Bryan Adams's '(Everything I Do) I Do It for You' get knocked off UK number one, its perch for the last four months of her life.

It seems blasphemous that my mother's death even existed in the same reality as those moments that subsequently came to define my youth; taking the long way home from Nixon's Corner so I could listen to *Kid A* twice, or poring over the lurid covers of horror paperbacks in a newly discovered corner of Foyle Street library. How is my mother's passing even part of the same universe that gave me the simple pleasures of ice cream after swimming lessons in William Street baths, or scenting the sun cream on girls' skin as they daubed polish on their outstretched, nonchalant nails. My life wasn't over from that point on. I'd laugh and cry and scream about borrowed jumpers, school fights, bomb scares, playing *Zelda*, teenage bands, primary-school crushes and yet more ice cream after yet more swimming lessons. I'd just be doing it without her. To some extent, I'd be doing it without a memory of her. The most dramatic moment of my life wasn't scored by wailing sirens, weeping angels or sad little ukuleles, nimbly plucked on lonely hillsides. Mammy's death was mostly signalled by tea, sandwiches, and an odd little boy in corduroy trousers, announcing it with a smile across his face.

2

Halloween

Considering Derry spent the latter half of the twentieth century beholden to the tremors of large, loud explosions, its inhabitants' fondness for fireworks is greater than you might imagine. None in the city are bigger or louder than those that come in late October, when Derry throws the biggest Halloween celebration on Earth. The entire city goes for it full-strength, with a whole weekend of parties and events, all of which are fully costumed. Office workers, postmen, supermarket cashiers, your bus driver, all taking part in the broad spectacle of public japery that takes over the entire city for at least a few days, and often a week or two beforehand.

Something in the region of 100,000 fancy-dressed people flood the streets for outdoor events, and this in a city with a population of 110,000. Ordinarily, Derry folk are stoical and dismissive, and have earned something of a reputation for being wary of grandstanding. There's an unspoken distrust of anyone attracting too much attention to themselves. It's likely

19

a survival tactic, from a time when people in Derry felt slightly less safe than they do now. There's a caginess to the city's older inhabitants likely baked in from the bad old days, when cultivating a healthy fear of outside attention was probably quite wise. One legacy of the Troubles for people my age is that we can't even attack our elders for being grumpy and churlish, since back when they were kids, they were all being stopped by police four times a day or dragged out of their homes by soldiers at 4 a.m. for having the wrong surname. I came into my teens when the worst of the Troubles was finally receding, but that queasy paranoia was still everywhere around. And I mean everywhere. I once called the library on Foyle Street, looking for a book of ghost stories.

'Hello, is this the Central Library?' I asked.

'*Depends*,' came the inscrutable and suspicious reply some moments later. '*Who's asking?*'

On balance, Halloween was not an ideal time to return to school after Mammy died, since for the teacher it meant explaining the nature of death to twenty small children in a room that was dressed like a haunted house. Like the lustre of those new corduroy trousers – long since dulled by mud and sick – the frenetic activity in our home had faded. As the heaviest traffic of well-wishers abated, we had been left to grieve in peace, but now we had to go out into the world again. God knows how my dad fared at work, having to negotiate his colleagues' well-meaning but gormless attempts at consoling a man who'd lost his wife and the mother of his eleven children. Although I'd say it's likely they weren't in a room filled with novelty cobwebs. If the question I had asked all those distraught mourners at my mother's wake sought a literal answer, I was to receive it many times over the coming months. *Everyone* would hear that Mammy died, and in case they hadn't, my teacher Mrs Devlin would be good enough to remind them.

Other than its being Halloween, the main thing I remember about that day was the kindness of a boy named Philo McGahern. I don't know that Philo and I ever had two conversations in all the time we knew each other, but he made such an impression that, three decades later, his name and face remain embedded in my memory. Philo was an unfortunate-looking child: drooping mouth, strangely large eyes and brittle, blond bristles that emerged from his head where hair should have been. He had a shiny face, which must have been due to an ointment or balm that gave off a medicinal, mentholated smell like an old lady's handbag. I presume it was for the skin condition that caused the steady fall of transparent flakes from his cheeks and chin. These settled on his school jumper in such volume that he had the permanent look of someone who'd just eaten a croissant lying down.

The teachers in my school all dressed up for Halloween itself, even the nuns. Witches and banshees were popular among the sisters, but I seem to remember Sister Francistine coming as the Bride of Frankenstein, complete with stacked black bouffant threaded with a shock stripe of purest white. This is still par for the course in Derry at Halloween. Novelty costume shops spring from nowhere to dominate the local high streets, fulfilling demand for bottom-tier dressing-up supplies. Sometimes existing premises will alter their entire business model in October, since it makes better financial sense for them to sell witches' hats and Donald Trump masks in those few weeks than, say, pets or insulin. You can't throw a tiny plastic pumpkin without hitting a sign advertising 'ice scream' or '2-for-1 Squeals', prices 'slashed', and long-gestating discounts being 'back from the dead'. At some point in the nineties, restaurants hit upon *gravey* as a pun, and it's one they still ride pretty hard. For the lazier proprietor, there's a near-ubiquitous emphasis on the fear that might be induced by special offers, and practically every storefront in town is daubed with a slogan like 'deals so good they're scary', which even by the standard of such things has always struck me as a dubious claim. My father is the only person I know regularly frightened by prices, and those only on the higher end.

There are, of course, those who go above and beyond the call of witches, ghouls and topical celebrities, and instead strike out on their own. More abstract variants of fancy dress became a highly sought-after niche within the circle of true believers, and a cult developed around increasingly outré and involved rig-outs. My sister Caoimhe was one such person. The year she dressed as a road was probably my own personal favourite; a long black dress with road markings down its length, flecked with toy cars, street signs and roadside shrubs. My little brother Conall once dressed as Jack Woltz from *The Godfather*, contriving an absurdly uncomfortable backpack that worked as a vertical bed, pillow, and bloody horse's head, in which he walked around all night. My friend Paudie spent weeks making a shower, complete with rectangular frame festooned with a plastic curtain and soap dish, his skin-tone bodysuit adorned with strategically placed artisanal lather he'd made from cotton balls. Even more alarming was the fact we bumped into two other people who'd made their own shower that evening.

I think my all-time favourite was the man I encountered wearing a long-haired wig, sandals and a kaftan. The kaftan was overlaid with a lacy bra, on to which he had crudely stapled two white bread rolls, or baps, to use the local parlance. I stopped him to ask what he was; Burger Christ? Breadroll Shepherd Boobs? He took a dramatic swig from his bottle of Buckfast, arcing it to his lips to prolong the moment with the cocksure swagger of a hair metal guitar solo. 'John the Bap Tits,' he said.

I don't know that I've ever been so impressed in my entire life.

Thankfully, Mrs Devlin wasn't costumed for her announcement, which came a few days before Halloween itself. She stood at the front of the class, and I beside her like a solemn little urchin, fumbling with my sleeves. Mrs Devlin had a commanding aura, one of those indomitable older women that you could imagine spending her bank holidays in a small static caravan in Donegal, doing thousand-piece jigsaws of Pádraig Pearse, or knitting balaclavas for the Provisional IRA. In appearance, she was effectively Little Old Lady #6 from a Central Casting extras catalogue, with a solid, shiny hive of nut-brown hair, a sharp, dropped mouth and am-dram whiskers on her pointed chin. Standing in heels, she was roughly 4' 11", and weighed about six stone soaking wet, perhaps five, discounting brooches and hairpins. If you picked her up and shook her by the boots, your carpet would shortly be littered with hankies, rosary beads and those minty sweets that smelled of Philo. She wore tortoiseshell glasses that were fixed about her neck with a chain, as if selected by a hungover costume supervisor who'd been given five seconds to dress a sketch in which an old lady complains about the soup in a three-star hotel. She rarely smiled or showed affection, but she'd spent the entire morning doing both as she held my hand.

She stalled for time. Growing up, I was fascinated by that moment you often see in American sitcoms, when popular characters would appear on stage but were unable to deliver their lines until the laughter caused by their arrival had died down. I'd always watch what they did as they stood there, silently vamping as they patted down their clothes or adjusted their hair, riding the wave of noise with eight or nine seconds of odd gestures that would have immediately marked you out as a psychopath had you acted that way in real life. I saw something of this in Mrs Devlin, who was choosing not to speak over the usual din, but waited until actual, real silence had prevailed. When it finally did, she fumbled and strained. Her mouth went slanted and she kept starting and stopping, as if her throat was a leaf-blower she couldn't get going.

'Class. This – Boys and girls. Séamas – This morning, Séamas has returned to class.'

She now alternated between clasping her hands in front of her and returning them to my scalp for nervous pats. I was still very much unenthused by physical affection, but had been effectively passed around like a stress toy for the preceding two weeks. Only now do I realise how hard my mother's death had been on these adults themselves, since they obviously cared about my welfare but were also extremely fond of my mother, who had died so young and left such tragedy behind her.

'Now, as some of you might know,' Mrs Devlin said, 'Séamas's mammy has just died, and he's very sad.' I had been smiling nervously, but now frowned, as if I was in a school play

24

about a sad little boy. 'Everyone should be extra nice to him, because you wouldn't like it if your mammy died, would you?' I held the frown, concentrating hard on the pose, the way you do while waiting for a photograph to be taken.

I don't know that I should have even been present for this, and wonder if they do things differently now. The whole thing felt rigid and strange. Maybe they had gone over it during the fortnight in which I was absent, and this was merely a reminder. Maybe repetition was necessary. Perhaps this public airing was itself a humane approach, a way of avoiding my mother's death becoming one of those half-known-but-unmentioned tragedies that were common currency among kids, and Northern Irish kids in particular. 'To save confusion in future, the following tragedies have occurred', that sort of thing. The alternative led to misunderstandings, and having to spell it out again and again to people who weren't aware.

'You wouldn't like it if your mammy died, would you?' seemed an odd sort of a way of putting it. It would, I argue, have been preferable for this not to have been phrased as a question, one with a somewhat flimsy, glib connotation, suggesting a debate could be had on the subject. Luckily, the mood of the room seemed clear: my classmates would not like it if their mammies died.

My memories are mostly of blank, gawping faces staring back at Mrs Devlin, but also, amid the glum silence, of slowly registering the artwork that adorned every wall: painted pumpkin handprints and gory blood-effect names rendered in red acrylic paints. The room was festooned with whimsical skeletons, tombstones and wispy joke-shop cobwebs emerging from the filing cabinet beside Mrs Devlin's desk, terminating eventually behind the long, thin poster of the alphabet that stretched just below the ceiling, at the other end of the room. Guys, you shouldn't have, I might have thought to myself upon seeing the entire room decked out with macabre tokens of death and horror. But I didn't, because I was five.

As I stood in front of my classmates, it occurred to me that they'd done all this decorating while I was away, and I felt that pang of melancholy one feels upon realising time has not stood still for others when it has done for you. My friends hadn't been at chilly gravesides, or home vigils, bouncing from one relative's knee to another while priests spoke low Latin in sing-song tones. They'd been drawing and cutting out jaunty pumpkins with their names on. This moment of transcendent solemnity, watched over by a dozen melted Homers Simpson, and malformed Sonics the Hedgehog, was broken only by heavy breathing from Philo, who then raised his hand. 'My granny died,' he said, in a rather touching show of solidarity-cum-one-upmanship. 'His granny died,' said Aoife, nodding to the room in agreement, as if this extraordinary claim required someone to vouch for it. She also said this while pointing at Philo, as if telling on him.

The room considered this exchange, and several classmates shared that their grannies had also died. Their grandas too, in some cases. Paul had suffered the loss of a turtle, some fish and three dogs, a litany of tragedy that had clearly been as painful for him as it was suspicious to us. It's odd to recall such earnest ruminations on death and grief being carried out among small children for whom the words meant little, and who would, in roughly twenty minutes, be wearing water-proof bibs and smacking jugs around sandpits. Handed a little red car, many of us could not yet be relied upon to sort it with all the other little red cars, but here, in that moment, the garishly coloured environs of 2B of Nazareth House Primary became the unlikely setting for a seminar on grief, and the first ever conversation for many of us about bereavement and how to handle it. I became a special correspondent from grief's remotest outpost, returning from uncharted land to tell everyone what I'd seen. Once a few questions had been asked, it was hard to stem the tide. My classmates began with solemn commiserations but, quite soon, graduated to slightly more probing queries.

'Did she go to heaven?'

'Do you get to visit her in heaven?'

'Will she bring back presents?'

'Like a Toblerone?'

'My uncle got one in Florida.'

'Is heaven in Florida?'

'Is there a Disneyland in heaven?'

'Does heaven have Toblerones?'

I answered each like a hurried politician on courthouse steps, unused to this degree of interest in my life. I was soon experiencing that first weird rush from the publicity that came with having 'the big news' in class. Being one of eleven had starved me of attention, and here it was being offered up to me in an undiluted and gravely significant form. My years of self-loathing were a long way away, so for now I rode that wave of attention like a piebald pony. Lacking the tact to package it any other way, my friends made it clear that my bereavement was to be rewarded.

'Would you like my milk, because your mum died?' offered

Philo, rather sweetly. 'Yes,' I must have answered, because I certainly drank that milk. I also got to feed the fish, use the crap little robot no one had ever really figured out how to work and generally do all the best things before everyone else.

It's easy to say the sadness I felt was incomprehensible, but I suppose that this was true in its most literal sense. I was incapable of comprehending what had changed, or that it had changed for ever. Death itself was too huge for me to grapple with, and my mother's death was, to me, only questionably permanent. Just recently, she wasn't dead; she held my hand and told me to play out in the trees by the hospital. Now she was dead, which meant she was happy and healthy, and therefore alive, but in heaven. Who knew what came next? Apart from anything else, the whole heaven thing seemed like a great deal for the time being. I have no memory of the specifics of what I imagined, I just knew that heaven was a real, physical place, and I couldn't visit her there. I was used to her being away, since she'd previously spent time in Belfast, where I *could* visit her, but it was made clear to me Belfast and heaven were different in that respect and several others.

Heaven became a source of fascination for me. I was ready to believe in heaven, since it seemed like a great place, and it made sense Mammy would end up there. If even eighty people in all time had made the grade, then my mother would have been one of them. The confusing thing was that people would tell me it was great that Mammy had gone there, but in a voice that didn't seem to suggest it was great at all, and was actually very sad. People would be fighting back tears while telling me the good news, the way people now might tell you how

28

proud they are that their child does improv comedy, or that their husband is getting his old band back together. It seemed as though these adults didn't realise that I could see them as they spoke, since their words were so at odds with their facial expressions. As a concept, heaven always seemed to lead to conversational cul-de-sacs that were uniquely unsatisfying for any five-year-old, let alone a boy genius like myself, famed for his interrogative skills. Heaven was great news, clearly, but so much more information was needed, and it stunned me that it wasn't forthcoming. When it comes to most positive news, people usually can't shut up about it, and will do anything to add more detail. It's a facile truth about people, that we like to rave about even mediocre experiences other people haven't yet been made aware of, like when people tell you that you should watch *Billions*, and you think of just how many other shows you would have to watch first to justify it, or that time you tried almond milk for a week and ended up, drunk, singing its praises to your taxi driver, before never drinking it again. Yet here I was being presented with what, on the face of it, seemed like the most incredible news of all time, the literal Good News that Christians love so much – death is not the end – delivered as if it was a terrible blow.

What makes it weirder is this was not just a convenient thing to say to a child, like Santa Claus being real or eating carrots being good for my eyesight. This was, and is, Catholic dogma, something these people professed to believe. Heaven is canon, it exists. And yet adults were being strangely evasive when it came to answering my numerous questions.

'What does she do there?' I'd ask. 'Does she teach?' I still have questions about what this version of heaven comprises to this day. What would Mammy look like there: her current self, thinner and scarred but alive? Or her younger self? Does she get to pick, like can she just opt for when she felt happiest or most attractive? If you're blind or deaf in life, can you see and hear in heaven? Wouldn't that be confusing? What do you wear in heaven? Do you have to wear the clothes you died in for all eternity? If John the Bap Tits was run over would he have to walk around in heaven for all time dressed in a bra with burger buns on? Or can you change your clothes up there? Are there shops? If so, who works in them? Do some people live a good enough life to get to heaven, only to arrive there and end up working in a shop? Other people playing harps all day on clouds and you end up working 9 to 5 in a Primark in heaven? Does heaven have countries and cities and buildings and cars? Can all people of all languages communicate? Are there people there from Neanderthal times? Can you have pets? Or does every living thing have to have had a soul? Do dogs make it there? If you die as a child do you stay that age in heaven for ever? Can you die in heaven and go to another, further heaven? Does Mammy get to watch us? How could she be happy if she knew we were suffering? Or if she watched us die and then saw that we didn't make it up there to see her?

People were kind to me, but couldn't answer any of these questions, and just the fact I'd asked these things appeared to be upsetting for them, as if they'd done something wrong in telling me about heaven in the first place. It was a lot like other times I'd ask awkward questions, like when I heard negligible nineties UK RnB hit 'Horny' by Mark Morrison and kept asking my dad – a man who may never have said the word out loud in his life – what horny meant, and whether he was himself horny. Another time I followed our housekeeper Anne around and asked her why someone would become a prostitute – a question I'd just heard Richard Madeley ask a guest on *This Morning*. Because I was just copying his vocal inflections, she took it for granted that I, despite being four, knew what I was asking, and tried her best to walk me through it.

Before long, though, I went back to my usual conversational fare: long-winded descriptions of dinosaurs, or the differences between various types of trees. At the end of my first full day back at school, Philo presented me with a picture of his granny and my mother in heaven together, surrounded by clouds. I thought it was great, and his inclusion of Paul's menagerie of expired pets was a beautiful touch.

I don't have very many memories of my mother. I do know that I dreamt about her a lot after she died. And those dreams were of us in heaven. The dreams were all the same, pretty much. They always took the form of a mundane visitation; she wouldn't be bathed in light or descending from the clouds. She would be normal, unheralded and domestic. In the dreams, she was never just there, in heaven; I would have to find her. I would know that she was gone, but hear her voice and know that she'd returned. This was never a big fanfare, but rather a commonplace discovery; hearing her voice speaking quietly from the kitchen, in the facsimile of our house that God had arranged for us to live in. Following her voice from the utility room into the back hall to turn the door and find her there, sitting at the table.

In the dream, she looks up but doesn't look at me, as if there will be plenty of time to look at me for ever now that we're reunited, and anyway she's doing something, mending a shirt or wetting a cloth to wipe away a smudge on a tiny little trouser leg. She's listening to something on the radio that I can't quite make out, but which she is enjoying because she's smiling, or perhaps humming along. They get BBC Radio Ulster in heaven. Of course they do. She, too, is hard to make out, since she is there and not there, as if seen through a fluttering sheet, and the room is swimming with the disjointed, various noise of dreams: the radio and the dishwasher; the dog just below us, where hot pipes warm the cold floor under our kitchen table. I can hear slow breathing, from the dog not my mother, and the light scrape of nails on linoleum. There might be other people in the room, but I can't see them through the fluttering sheet, and in any case they're not taking much notice of her. She just is, and I can tell she's in no hurry, because she's so busy with what she's doing. She's humming and mending and fiddling with ordinary things. She's not bestowed with cosmic grace and ready to give me koans from the afterlife. She's reading a magazine, or putting some Mass cards in a box, or sticking her tongue out ever so slightly as she threads a needle. She's doing the sorts of things that living people, living *mammies*, do.

Sometimes the dream ends with me deciding to go to some other room and fetch her something, something to get her attention, something that will make her remember me. The second I leave, the second even that I look away, she's gone. I've torn my mother from myself by taking my eye off her. By taking her for granted, again. I threw her away, and it's my fault. Other times, dream logic is suspended and I'm fully aware of the precariousness of my situation. I must steadfastly keep her in sight without breaking concentration. And these times, something else, some ineffable paralysis, still manages to get in the way. I'm not scared, I know that everything is fine, but I also know that she's dead, and this moment is finite. I know and I don't know. As I come closer it's as if the sheet in front of my face flutters even more frantically, as if my brain is buffering from the emotional load of gazing at her head-on. My mother is no longer someone I can look at directly, but peripherally only, like the sun, or one of those fences that have backward slats so you can only see through into the garden beyond if you're walking past quite quickly.

From what I can see of her, she's happy, and I can tell that getting to see me again is a kindness to her. She speaks, but the things she says are too quiet for me to hear above the radio and the dog and the dishwasher. I strain my ears and try to focus on her lips, but I can't hear her properly and I can't go to her, I can't be with her, because there's something holding me back, as if I'm wading, shin-height, through fruitcake mix. I decide I don't even need to hear her speak; I just want to reach her so I can be held, and so I can tell her I wish she was back, whether she hears me or not, whether she's real or not; I want to tell her that I'm sad and I don't understand, and that none of this makes any sense. I want to tell her how sad we all are, and how sad it makes each of us to know how sad the rest of us are. We don't know what to do, and we don't even know if we're making each other worse.

But I also don't want to say a thing, I don't want her to be sad, I don't even want her to know that she's dead and how sad that makes me. I just want her to hold me in the normal way of living people. The sheet is fluttering, and the noise continues, and my feet are moving so slowly, too slowly, I'm just trying to get to her, trying to make it to the point where she can pick me up, where I can sit on her lap and feel her close and know again how it is to be held by someone whose heart isn't breaking.

3

Mother's Day

I first realised I'd erased my mother when I was eight. It was Mother's Day 1994. Mother's Day was always kind of a drag, but not for the reason you might imagine. It was just a bit awkward, teachers becoming nervy and sheepish when it was coming up, nibbling on fingernails, fiddling with bracelets, staring at me like some tea they'd gulped without checking if the milk was in date. For a week or so, I'd be the unwilling recipient of weak smiles and tender shoulder pats from ordinarily taciturn figures, all of whom were, like Mrs Devlin, stern little women with Derry accents that could rust a bike. Now they were suddenly tiptoeing about me like I was a sad little ginger landmine.

What's weird is that throughout this time when people were walking on eggshells, I was aware that what they feared saying around me were invariably bland, generalised things that never could have hurt me. Mother's Day, first communion, confirmation, and other such events at which my mother would have been present, I simply didn't associate with her, since no tradition of her attendance had been established. Playground gaffes affected me even less. I've lost count of the times an ill-placed 'your mum' joke would be deployed before its issuer remembered I was Séamas of the Dead Mam, and a whole tedious spiral would kick off: first a collective 'oooooooooooh, that's lousy!' would erupt from the others, and then my antagonist's face would drop in a paroxysm of horror. At this point any hypothetical disagreement I had with the person was shelved, and I'd immediately shift gears to downplay the insult, since this interaction was always more annoying and painful than any supposed slight might have been. It was never any use. 'Shit. I'm sorry, I didn't—' they'd splutter and cringe, while I'd do my best to reassure them, which always made them feel worse. They often cried themselves, like they were putting a hex on their own mums. They wouldn't like it if their mam died, after all. Some things were no joking matter, and my mum was one of them, but I never really understood even this. The mum in a 'your mum' joke wasn't a real thing, it wasn't my mum. I once even tried to put this across by explaining that Mammy couldn't have been so fat she had her own postcode, since she was skinny even before she got cancer. This made things much worse, and I never tried that strategy again.

As with Mother's Day, it seemed that people who hadn't grieved didn't know what could make me sad. It felt alienating to realise that they still had such a Fisher-Price imagining of what it was like. The idea that my grief could be sullied by something as innocuous as a fat mam joke was almost blasphemous, and stuck with me more than any such joke ever could itself. What made their inability to empathise all the more clear was the freedom with which they constantly slandered their own mums, assaulting them with language more commonly used by dock workers if they didn't get what they wanted for Christmas, or weren't allowed to go out that weekend. It was those moments that stung me into sullen silence in the canteen, and would recur during fitful sleepless nights, the callousness with which they set fire to the feast they held in their hands while I looked on and starved.

So, no, I didn't care about Mother's Day. I didn't understand why I was even supposed to. That this day was supposed to be especially painful for me was just one more indicator that none of these adults had a clue. It seemed crass, even at eight, that a pain so profound could be altered by the date on the calendar, a day that seemed so impersonal and silly and had nothing to do with my mother or our relationship. On the day itself, I didn't mind the fuss, since it usually meant I'd be left to my own devices. While everyone else was getting high on maternal love, glue and finger-paints, the teachers would freeze and I'd get to read in the corner.

When I was eight, however, I did actually do something. Everyone was making sparkly cards. Kev was so overzealous with the glitter that the only thing he gifted his mother that year was an evening under a desk lamp, digging sparkly gunk from around his weeping eyeballs. The classroom was quiet, aside from the soft, slow snipping of those stumpy little scissors they give kids, the blue plastic ones with all the bite of a damp oven glove. It was to this soundtrack I remember sitting in the corner, having tasked myself with writing a list of every memory I had of my mother.

Straining from the effort, I wrote down ten. Ten clear

memories. My internal accounting had fooled me into thinking my stock was larger than it was. I could cycle through them in my head and never bother keeping count, and ten was about enough that I had never realised how small the number was. Writing them down made it clear just how little of her I had left. I felt bereft. Worse still, I never kept that list and, years later, realised with horror that the best I could manage was five. At the point at which I started writing this book, that was all I had. I'd not been paying attention and I'd deleted half of my mother from myself. Losing yet more of Mammy felt like a second bereavement.

Whatever stock of memories I had of Mammy in the first place, I'd steadily got used to losing, without being aware that it was happening, or thinking to do something to stop it. I sometimes wonder if my impulse to read everything, know everything and broadcast to everyone all of these wonderful everythings I knew, well into my teens, was all about beating the encroaching darkness of things forgotten, about proving that I would and could never let my guard down again. The boy who knew everything couldn't possibly have forgotten his own mother.

The memories I have left are patchy and fleeting, but can still rise, fully formed. They're not particularly impressive or spectacular; they're the kind of homespun everyday things that shouldn't really have stuck around.

1. I am in a car, Mammy's car, and we're driving down Abercorn Road.
I have no idea when this would have been, since I can't place my own age, but we're on our own in Mammy's horrible

old Datsun, a white car in the shape of a loafer that would subsequently grow old and mossy in the little parking area around the back of the house, behind the kitchen. There's music on the radio. My knees are pressed up near my chest, because like all little boys I am locked in a constant, futile cycle of actions designed exclusively to be scolded for. She is telling me to put them down, and placing her left hand on mine for a moment, before changing gear. She is humming along to the radio, which is playing 'Eternal Flame' by the Bangles. She is still smiling from something just said by the presenter before the song began. I feel like we were travelling from William Street, but we could have been coming from Nazareth House on Bishop Street, or our parish church of St Columba's, Long Tower.

2. I am shouting at her on my birthday.

I suppose it would make sense that it's my fifth. I am sitting in the kitchen with my friends around me, and Daddy to my right. I have, bless my little heart, become a little over excited by the day's events and, in that constant way of children's birthday parties, reduced myself to something bestial and cruel, a godless little horror. I believe I have just witnessed someone eating some of my cake before I'd got a chance to, and decreed this to be the last mistake they'd make on this highest of high holy days. I scream at them to stop, and all my little friends are looking at each other, or suddenly seem quite fascinated by their fingernails. Mammy, quite understandably, remonstrates with me about being nicer to my friends, and I scream in her face, quite forcefully because she doesn't understand me, birthdays, or cake.

3. She is coming in to pick me up from school.

I am in reception class, with Mrs Hartop, and being allowed
to continue playing at the table where you sort things by
shape or colour while all the other kids are packing up and
going home. I'm afforded this extra few minutes because
my mother is catching up with Mrs Hartop. They are both
laughing and smiling, and Mrs Hartop grabs my mother's
arm at one point in that 'oh no, stop it' way you sometimes
do to emphasise how little you want someone to stop it. They
are at the back of the class, and I am proud that Mammy
knows the teacher so well, because none of the other parents
talk to her at all. She sticks out her hand in a wordless gesture
that means we're going and as I cradle my head to her knee
she tells me to say goodbye.

4. We are on a bus on Bishop Street.

My mother is carrying shopping bags, and the plastic handles
are digging into her fingers. The bus has either stopped for
a long time, or has just been interrupted by the army. We
are at the bottom end of Bishop Street, with the river on
our left and Moore Walk on our right, just before the turn
toward the dump, and the Brandywell. It's a bright, sunny
day, and there is a bomb somewhere on the road. The sunlight is coming in the window at such an angle that I have to
cup my hand slightly over one eye to see the driver, who is
talking to a soldier through the window. He looks bothered
but not upset. Mammy, looking worried, puts her shopping
down and holds my hand very tight. She is chewing her
thumbnail. There are two more soldiers outside, not looking in but talking to each other; both are carrying machine

guns, and are beside two armoured cars in which sit several other soldiers. There is a woman at the front of the bus, near the driver, who jokes with him after the soldier departs. We are not allowed to leave the bus. Instead we reverse back up Bishop Street until we can turn and take a detour some way back. I say the words 'bomb scare' for days afterwards.

5. She is dancing with Daddy.

We're all in the kitchen with Mammy, when Daddy enters with a rose, or bouquet of roses, for Mammy. It's Valentine's Day or their anniversary or something, and he gives her a decidedly PG kiss on the cheek as he presents the flowers, with great theatricality for our benefit. Groans of displeasure ring out as he does so, and he takes delight in the sincere mortification evoked by his showing Mammy affection. Emboldened, he places a rose between his teeth like a crooning heart-throb and affects a Lothario facial expression, all arched eyebrows and tilted head. He takes Mammy by the hand and leads her around the kitchen, cheek to cheek, in an improvised waltz, the rose still in his mouth. There are squeals of laughter, and he sings something schmaltzy and adoring into her ear. Mammy is blushing and laughing, and I am screaming with delighted horror.

6. I am eating a Penguin bar.

It's a Friday. Mammy has got off early, maybe. Someone is early, I can feel that for sure. It's me, Fionnuala and Conall, the three youngest. We are sitting at the giant kitchen table, with a Penguin bar each and some lemonade. This is a party. It's special, because Mammy doesn't usually let us have chocolate or fizzy drinks, but on Fridays before the school ones come in, we have this little treat among ourselves. Mammy is asking us about our days, genuinely interested to know what we've been up to.

7. We are sitting in a caravan.

We're in Westport, Mayo, and Mammy and I are sitting in the caravan, the old caravan that is too small for all of us but seems perfect for just us two. My friend Andrew and his mother are here too, because they've been staying in the same caravan park, and it was a surprise that they are there, and his mum comes in. They are speaking quietly in the back part, while we play with toys at the table to the side, both very confused as to how friends from school have somehow appeared, fully formed, 150 miles from our usual haunt, across a border where accents are unfamiliar and even the sweets are different. It is nine or ten at night, the light is dimming, and one or both of us has been woken up to see the other, so we can play while they chat. Mammy and Mrs McIvor are friends because they gave birth to us in adjacent hospital beds, he arriving three hours after me. Mammy is talking about hospitals again, and smiling for Mrs McIvor, and saying that things are in God's hands. Mammy's hands are in Mrs McIvor's, who has clasped them between the handkerchief she's been using to wipe her eyes.

8. She is in her bedroom.

It must be early in the morning, because the curtains haven't been opened yet. Daddy isn't in the room, so he may be in the kitchen or has already left for work. I've come into their room to find Mammy placing small foam pads in the front of her dress. The relative murk in the room is accented by two or three ineffably small slivers of sunlight that slice, wafer-thin, through the dark curtains. Mammy is not remotely fazed at seeing me come in, and as I sit on their bed she carries on, saying something to me I can't place, as she sprays some perfume on her wrists and neck. I see the individual drops of the perfume ascend as motes of dust, as they pass over her shoulder and through the sunbeams poking through the window.

You may have noticed that there were more memories there than the five I previously mentioned. This is because, over the course of writing this book, three more have resurfaced, bringing the total to a slightly more respectable eight. Even light reading on the subject suggests that memories are scarcely trustworthy things, so I don't really know how many of these are fully real recollections drawn from focusing on aspects of my life that were too painful to consider for the past three decades, or half-fudged fakes contrived from going over other people's stories and looking at old photographs.

When people say memory is treacherous, I think it's truer even than they intend. They usually mean treacherous the way Irish weather forecasters describe rainy roads or windy hills: as in unreliable, not to be counted on. They're right, of course. Your brain can't be relied upon to give you a full account of the things you lived through last week, let alone twenty or thirty years ago. When writing invoices for freelance work, I frequently put down the address not of my last apartment, but the one from two house moves ago, where I haven't lived in nearly half a decade. I have several times been looking at pictures from a friend's day out or birthday party and commented on how great the venue looks, even asking my wife if we can go there some time. It is then that I swipe one photo to the right and find myself, at that event with all those people, likely talking about how nice it is there. There's a painting in my brother's house that I have complimented, in effusive terms, as really livening up the place and showing a bold new direction for the sitting room's decor, at least three times in the past two years. This would be slightly less maddening if it weren't for the silence said painting has generated the other dozen or so times I've stood in that room. When it comes to ancient memories, especially those from childhood, it's hard to know if you're remembering the thing, or what you've been told to remember about that thing; suggested glimpses at the distant past, over which each subsequent re-tread is tracing thicker and thicker lines of falseness.

Every time you remember something, an imperceptible inaccuracy percentage creeps in, meaning the more you remember an event, a place, even a person's face, the less reliable the memory will be. I got it in my head that my schoolmate Paul looked a bit like Boris Becker, and was surprised to discover how little I recognised him twenty years later, as my brain had slowly eroded every bit of information I once had about his face that wasn't Becker-shaped. The longer you leave things, the more time these subsequent recollections have to spread the reproduction errors, carrying those extra added untrue details which, once insignificant, aggregate into a greater portion of the whole.

Memory is, however, also treacherous in that other, more

sinister sense of the word. As I grew older, I felt that having forgotten so much of my mother made me a bad and unfeeling son, and the shame of deleting her from myself screwed into my brain, dripping poison where it went. Maybe this is why I ended up with so few memories – it hurt to remember, and in neglecting to do so, the road less travelled receded back into the bush. Years afterwards, I grieved Mammy in the more normal ways, and memories of the gormless naivety with which I conducted myself would be exquisitely painful. By ten or eleven, I would look back on this time constantly, locked into repetitive feelings of shame and remorse. I'd force myself to relive memories, like a tongue seeking the siren pain of a shaky tooth. I'd remember, too, how I capitalised on the attention I got for being a newly minted half-orphan. Maybe this is why, at some point, I stopped remembering those things, and so many of the times we had together drifted away.

Most people seem prepared to treat their memories shabbily, to consign them to a cavernous dustbin in their brains, never sought or ordered, only to be touched when necessary. Having deleted so much of my mother, I realise I started to undertake a rather different approach. I began to remember everything, holding my memories close and repeating them to myself, writing things down when necessary, but mostly savouring life as it happened in real time. I would not have the same thing happen to me again. Now, my memories would be put to work. I started to amass knowledge in a way that was avaricious and obsessive. And incredibly annoying. One time I asked my Uncle Frank if he knew what deciduous meant, so he humoured me by saying he didn't. This was a cruel, cruel trap on my part, for I subsequently followed him around his own house making fun of him for his ignorance. There are dozens of stories like this from my childhood, so it would be handy if I could attribute this kind of behaviour to my bereavement. It makes for a sad picture, but on the plus side, it does let me off the hook when, to be honest, there's just as good a chance I was merely a precocious dork whose mam had died.

I have extraordinarily detailed memories of how people treated me when they discovered Mammy was dead, how differently they spoke to me. Throughout my school years, indiscreet acquaintances would tell me how much their parents would talk about my family, using us as a devastating example for them to live up to, as if our experience were a cautionary tale to be shared round the dinner table. 'You're lucky you have your mother,' they'd bark over salty gammon. 'For God's sake, poor critters over there, I don't know how it is they cope at all.' It was worse being fussed over by mams in person, of course. They'd fidget and mumble and laugh at everything I said. Often, they would buy me things for no reason. They'd ask about my dad a lot, and say how wonderful we all were, and him especially, but in a tone that suggested it was simply miraculous we hadn't beaten ourselves to death with lead pipes from all the grief. Older Irish women possess an uncanny ability to fear nothing so much as causing offence, while being so clumsily, dependably offensive it would almost be better they never spoke at all. One time, Colum Dineen's mum was driving me home when she quietly said, 'You're all great,' while crossing herself, as if my family's experience was itself contagious, a harbinger of death against which was needed specific and ritualistic protection right there and then. I was, in some sense, every parent's nightmare, personified in a bookish lad hammering them with facts about *Star Wars*, or long division, or spiders, and wondering, in between big greedy bites on the way back from football training, why I'd been bought an entire mid-journey box of chocolates in the first place.

Lacking the memories to form a coherent sense of Sheila O'Reilly in my head, I relied instead on what I could see of her around me, specifically all the times I'd see her each day. She was the giant, lovely photograph in the good room, and the smiling face in a few other family portraits throughout the house. She was the printed-out brochures for her anniversary Masses, and the small laminated Mass cards that were placed in a few of the bedrooms. I realise now she was becoming a fragmentary presence; more an idea, or set of loosely positive values, than a human being. I think people presumed I remembered more than I did, and I was too ashamed to admit that I didn't, so I would gamely agree each time teachers told me that Mammy wouldn't like this or that bold thing I'd done, or would have been proud of me for others. I was often told incredibly specific things about her that I didn't know where to put.

'Your mother *hated* coffee ice cream,' my dad might say, offering a delightful little garnish of detail for my older siblings, an extra bit of colour to add to the full and complex idea of Mammy they had in their heads. For us Wee Ones, however, such details were a different prospect. We didn't have the same store of detail, so the fact that she hated coffee ice cream, loathed *Home and Away*, or adored the two-penny slot machines in Bundoran would attain undue prominence, since these might be the twelfth or thirteenth facts we knew about Mammy in total. By the time I was seven, I'd forgotten what Mammy's voice sounded like, but would pepper people with jarringly irrelevant facts about her to convince them, and myself, that I remembered her well.

'I knew your mother,' a nurse once said to me as she administered a jab in school. I was seven and, as ever, glad to hear someone praising her, so nodded as she withdrew the needle and dabbed my arm with cotton.

'She really was a wonderful woman,' she continued, with touching sincerity.

'Yeah, she was,' I agreed, before adding, meaningfully, '*and allergic to bees, of course.*'

My confusion around her really was at its apex around that time, when I was preparing for my first holy communion, and kept finding it hard not to picture Mammy as the Virgin Mary, the way it's hard to read *One Flew Over the Cuckoo's Nest* without doing the same for Jack Nicholson as Randle McMurphy. She just fitted the part: a beautiful, sinless woman to whom people were devoted, and who spent her days now gazing, head tilted in silent stillness, from Catholic walls. Mammy had left traces of course, beyond the little tics and facial similarities people would spot here and there in each of us. She was the rapidly decaying scent of herself in the Datsun behind the house, and the sing-song cadence of the grace we said before meals. She was the daffodils in the garden, and the prayer pinned above the TV in the kitchen. More specifically, she was the text of this prayer itself, since she had written it out in crispest Loreto script.

The fact it was handwritten seemed to bind her that little bit more than the words themselves, and left us unwilling to remove the prayer – written hurriedly on red construction paper and intended to be temporary – for over a decade after she died, preferring instead to let it became increasingly tattered, steam-stained and ravaged by the travails of a working kitchen. When it finally did come down, it seemed like a tiny little fraction of her memory went with it, but it really was too grimy to remain. I think it was the chip pan, mostly, that did an even worse job on the other major wall adornment of that time, a soiled Garfield cuddly that hung, arms outstretched, like an irreverent feline Christ. It bore a spatula, fork and irretrievably yellow-tinged apron that declared MY KITCHEN, MY RULES, barely readable due to the layer of chip fat in which it was coated. I suppose I miss them both.

I don't know how I felt in the early days. I probably had it easier than my older siblings, who had to work through the whole gamut of abandonment, depression and anger when they had a little more emotional intelligence and so felt it harder. I just know that by the time I was old enough to piece together an idea of my mother as a whole, complex person, the details I had to go on weren't particularly whole or complex. Occasionally, like that nurse, people would spot who I was and tell me about her. A guy in Baldies' Barber on Castle Street kept me there for half an hour telling me about how much she meant to everyone in Foyle Hospice, an institution she ardently supported. My friend Eoghan's uncle stopped in his tracks to buy me a pint when he discovered Sheila, an old teaching colleague of his, had been my mother. He took me aside and insisted she was the finest woman he ever met in his life and teared up with pride when he heard we were all doing so well, as if we were a basket full of puppies he now knew to have safely crossed a treacherous ravine.

She didn't teach in the secondary school I attended, but a lot of the teachers there had known her, either through my older brothers, or because teachers generally seem to know each other in small cities. Occasionally one of them would stop me after class and give me a halting oration on her particular qualities, as when Mr Costigan held me lightly at the shoulder as everyone else filed out of my first day in his class. 'The word I'd use to describe her is grace,' he said, with a faraway look in his eye, once all the other boys had left. 'She had an extraordinary grace and compassion to her that you just don't see in many people.' I loved hearing these things and would sit and savour every last word. It happened quite a lot. Derry people are quite forward, of course, but it is also a testament to how much she meant to so many people, and how much her death affected them. 'She was one of God's angels, Sheila O'Reilly,' one woman said as she stopped me in the central library. I was trying to walk out with some books I hadn't rung in at the time. 'Sure as anything, she was.' They spoke as though she was a saint, which I obviously liked, but which also made her seem strangely remote. I longed to get a sense of who she was as a person, as a real, breathing person, beyond her intense dislike for an Australian soap, bees and coffee ice cream.

As I got older, I realised there were other people's memories that could fill the gaps, and having heard all the tales of how wonderful she was – and she really was – I found that I delighted more in hearing the scant few negative stories I could wring out of those who knew Mammy best. I spent my adolescence seeking out those corners of family events where they would be uttered like blasphemies through boozy breath and glinted eye: of how she could be holier-than-thou, that she could never get jokes right, how she couldn't write a story to save her life. Best of all was that beautiful evening I heard my mother's friend Patricia – in her glorious, mouth-bending, mid-Fermanagh twang – describe my mother's singing voice as 'sufficiently awful to disprove the existence of Gaww-id'.

Telling old stories is a large percentage of what we do when we return home. We sit around the huge kitchen table, which contained us comfortably back when our feet dangled inches from the floor. Even at full stretch, our fingers wouldn't reach its centre unless we leaned far enough forward that our chins pressed against its cold surface. These days we barely get round it at all. The whole thing creaks when we laugh. We do still fit, but if you need to nip to the toilet or grab another bottle from the garage, it's often easier to escape by slipping underneath and through a hedge-tight bramble of legs shaking with laughter than to inch past all those backs, pressed flat against the wall-seats lining either corner. Around that table, no one finishes a sentence, and we delight in each other's misremembered notions, undigested memories, embarrassing acts from the past – recollections of Mammy, of each other, of ourselves. It's there that the story of me at Mammy's wake will be endlessly relitigated. Only I'll be told I used slightly different wording, or actually it was only for a few minutes, or no, it was way worse and I was leaping around the place in full song. When corrected, I'm sure I intend to change my internal records, but those newer details rarely stick. We each long ago settled on our favourite tales, and each retelling grips them tighter to our tongues. We appreciate the preciousness of our own stock of memories, and perhaps there's no harm in jealously guarding them, safe from anyone who'd take away whatever clutch we have left. Laughing in those wee small hours, we rinse away with wine our shame for all the silly stories that we tell ourselves.

4

Numbers

There's a story my family tells around Christmas. As kids, that time of year was obviously pretty manic, but made more so by the fact each of us fancied ourselves as having prominent careers in showbusiness. We all sang in choirs at one time or another, and some of us in several at the same time.

I was less involved than most, yet even I sang in choirs for at least ten years, and the Christmas period was a time of constant shuttling between different masses or meetings or festive performances. Most of us were then also in school shows, nativities or orchestra recitals, and in the run-up to Christmas, a few of us even did the fully produced commercial pantos in town. I somehow never made the cut for those things, which I found odd because my kind eyes and easy way with people reminded many of a young Marlon Brando.

In any case, quite aside from the rigmarole of cooking and presents and the management of infant expectations that Christmas would demand from a single parent of eleven children, my father was rushed off his feet getting us to and from these various functions, and dealing with the preparations for overlapping performances. Walking through our house over Christmas was like a trip through the Warner Bros. lot in late-seventies Hollywood, only instead of showgirls and spacemen there would be assembled children dressed in their Sunday best, or as shepherds, or in the costume of some brutally crowbarred topical character favoured by school plays at the time. Many will remember my delighted turn as Reuben, the inexplicably French brother in *Joseph and the Amazing Technicolor Dreamcoat*, not least for my having done the entire thing dressed as Eric Cantona.

The main event was our primary school choir performing Christmas carols in old folks' homes and hospices, out of some misguided belief that the reedy timbre of our childish voices would provide balm to the elderly and dying. I remember finding the experience nice, in a way, although it was hard to gauge reactions since their clapping was generally quite slow and methodical, and having been told not to stare at the people with tubes connected to them, we decided to not look at anyone at all. My dad would be waiting for us to be done so he could take us home or, more likely, drive to the next place for another of us who was due at a similar engagement. It was actually worse if you didn't have anything to do, since you'd still be going all over the place and waiting in the car while everyone else was performing, which was way more boring than singing 'Frosty the Snowman' to the infirm. One of those Christmassy mornings, my brother Shane was singing at three Masses in a row. That's the 10, the 11 and the 12:15. After each, my dad would talk to a few fellow parishioners here and there, and pick up others of us who were at other Masses or concerts nearby. Owing to the comings and goings, headcounts got twisted, and on the drive back Shane turned round, surveyed the contents of the minibus and noticed that Dearbhaile was missing. She had been there in the chapel after the service, but had obviously stayed too long chatting to a friend and Daddy, understandably frazzled and depleted, had taken off without realising she wasn't on board.

He turned tail and raced back to the church to pick her up. He was furious. 'How did none of you notice she was missing?' he fumed, and everyone felt chastened at their lack of awareness, imagining her now crying on the steps of the church alone, or worse, in the company of scandalised and judgemental parishioners – or clergy – wringing their hands, apt to be telling tales very soon about the poor, rudderless O'Reilly clan, demented by grief, incapable even of counting themselves. When the bus finally reached Dearbhaile, however, she was smiling and happy, and neither in the company of some sour-faced scold among the congregation, nor alone.

I was standing there, unmissed, beside her.

Having lived in more normal-sized social environments since leaving home, a lot of my childhood seems as insane to me as it might to an outsider. I grew well used to separating out the many personalities in my family, discerning how each interacted with the others, how they formed into groups or reacted to the groups of others, but when I actually think about the ordinary, daily life we led, I find myself asking the same questions strangers ask. How did any of us get to use a bathroom in the mornings? When did Daddy sleep? Were we ever actually alone?

Every single evening for the first ten years of my life, I spent some part of it with at least nine of my siblings, in one house. We are similar enough in ages that we now all feel like peers, but I have to make myself remember that, as children, the age disparities were sufficient to make each of us feel we had little in common with at least half of our siblings. This was, I'm sure, more pronounced for the eldest three, the Big Ones, who must have felt put upon by the babysitting demands that fell on them precisely when they felt least like looking after children. Few tasks could be less appetising to a freshly minted teen than supervising one of six or seven younger siblings who held them in varying states of awe. I don't have to intuit this, since they said it quite openly all the time. When Dara and Shane were smashing themselves up on BMXs and sneaking fags, I was still using the tiny blue scissors to cut out pictures of dinosaurs that I could put in the cereal box of prehistoric bits and bobs I termed, rather grandly, my dinosaur den. I was as ignorant of their lives as I was of taxes, politics, or girls – although, in between snips, I do recall wondering why the latter's bums went all the way round. Despite this, at my father's insistence, I spent an inordinate amount of time with my older brothers. They already had to share a room with my little brother and me, which was probably not ideal, since when they were sixteen and fourteen years old, we were six and three, sleeping at the bottom of two bunk beds placed side by side. The room therefore operated on two different strata; on the top level, talk of football and fights and discos and illegal fireworks, while Conall, on the lower level, would be getting very detailed explanations about the dinosaurs I would point out to him – but never let him touch – in the snazzy cereal box he doubtless coveted.

Dara and Shane were charged with taking me into town or to football matches, probably just to give everyone a reprieve from my manic energy. They were less than thrilled about being seen in public with a small, strange ginger boy, and the fact that I carried around a box of dinosaur-related miscellany probably didn't help. But take me they did, and I almost always returned home safely. It's a curious thing that when time came for me to greet fatherhood at the age of thirty-two, I fretted a lot about whether I possessed the maturity and will to look after a child. I'd forgotten that so much of the guardianship I experienced in childhood was from children who actively resented my company. And in return I loved them more than anything.

I was well into adulthood before I realised most other people don't have to list their family in one long run, and always in age order – Sinead-Dara-Shane-Orla-Maeve-Mairead-Dearbhaile-Caoimhe-Fionnuala-Conall – because they will, otherwise, leave someone out. Even though this is true, I still reserve the right to be offended if anyone asks if I know all my siblings' names, which happens roughly a third of the time I mention the size of my family.

'Well,' I'll say, to some friend of a friend, in between bites of tapas, 'there is one brother whose name I've never caught.'

'Really?'

'Yeah, tall guy, lovely fella all things considered,' I'll say, spooning the last bit of tapenade onto a pitta, 'but it's just gone on too long. I'd feel rude introducing myself now that we're all approaching middle age.'

As children, our family's internal subdivisions were useful for keeping track of the different age groups. Like all class systems, it was instituted by those at the top, ostensibly as a shorthand for keeping things in order, while also conferring a certain irrefutable status on those who invented it. Being a Big One was just different from being a Middle One, no matter how old you got. Their seniority travelled with them, as if it were a ladder of power pulled up behind them as they climbed, out of reach to those who followed. Sinead, Dara and Shane were aristocrats, custodians of an unearned but unimpeachable moral authority that was rarely challenged or even considered, least of all by me, a Wee One through and through. Each of them had already left home for university by the time I started secondary school, an absence that only added to their cachet. The Big Ones had, after all, lived through that odd period of time when our family was relatively small, and watched first hand as it ballooned. To me this meant they might as well have been present at the birth of the Universe.

The Middle Ones, though only slightly younger in real terms, lacked this perspective, and so we held them in less awe. But they also knew the game was rigged. Unbeknownst to us at the bottom, at some point closer to the dawn of time the Big Ones had told Maeve and Orla that after a certain point – say, finishing primary school, or making your confirmation – a Middle One would progress to being a Big One. In reality, as each milestone came and went it became clearer and clearer that the divides were impermeable, and no such social mobility was possible. By the time this betrayal was realised, the Big-Middle-Wee heuristic had been intractably established. So much so, in fact, that when the Wee Ones reached those same milestones seven years later, it was with no concept that such a promotion was even being denied. Fuelled by resentment toward their social betters, the Middle Ones thus contrived deep distinctions between themselves and those below. In so far as four members of a family arbitrarily grouped together by age can be said to have an ethos, theirs might have been something like 'we are not Wee Ones'. Maeve and Orla set the rota in which our daily labours were enshrined. Dearbhaile, closest in age to the Wee Ones, and perhaps nervous this would place her position at risk, was particularly vigilant, and took to policing our bedtimes with the iron fist of a prison camp guard. These were delineated in increments, informally attached to the Australian soap operas they followed each weeknight. It was generally agreed that even the dewiest babe-in-arms should be permitted to stay up until the day-glo charms of *Neighbours* finished at 6 p.m. Staying up to watch the slightly more self-serious *Home and Away* was a privilege enjoyed only by those over twelve. The true Rubicon for emotional maturity was being allowed to watch *Heartbreak High*, which owed its place as our natural watershed to the fact that some of its characters had nose rings and disliked school. At each of these shows' end there would be an audible swivel of heads, as attention was brought to bear on whosoever had not yet decamped to their respective rooms for the evening. Were one of us Wee Ones bold enough to stay up later than was allowed, it was presumed we would be murdered, probably by Dearbhaile. Perhaps only Mairead didn't seem especially bothered by the ins and outs of who was where or what, maybe because she was technically the Middle Child and free from such insecurities. Although one does wonder if her placing merits the traditional distinction, when middle here means being the sixth of eleven.

For our part, being a Wee One meant being subject to a sort of benign servitude, but also free from the politicking that came from finding oneself so close to and yet so far from real power. We enjoyed a lessening of responsibility born of the fact that we were more likely to be considered, essentially, giant babies than functioning people, and this well into our older years.

We also benefited in another, less immediately obvious way. It's inarguable that my father relaxed with age, gradually loosening the grip in which he held his children as each managed to survive school trips, hospital visits, exam schedules and nights out without being maimed, murdered or featured in newspaper articles in which neighbours said we 'always seemed perfectly normal before this'. As younger parents, Mammy and Daddy adhered to a strict code that was largely absent by the time I was growing up. In fact, the televisual rubric I just described would have been unthinkable while my mother was still alive. She was not a lover of television, unlike my father, who loves the medium so much I'm pretty sure he can still see the 5USA logo when he shuts his eyes. It's likely that *Neighbours* became the staple of our TV diet since it was originally the only show that Mammy permitted us to watch, and even then only at lunch time during school holidays. It was supplemented by *Glenroe*, a gently diverting rural melodrama that ran on Sunday nights in Ireland for two decades on a budget roughly equivalent to a tube of Pringles. For me and every other Irish child, it was the last thing we were allowed to watch each weekend. Once we heard the strangled fiddle music that brought each episode to a close, we'd have to face the trudge towards bed, and the school week ahead. Which meant we'd sit through thirty minutes of crag-faced people in wellies having affairs near barns just to keep our weekend alive.

My parents had been stricter in other, more meaningful ways too. The Big Ones describe their adolescent years as if they were parented by the Stasi. Each tells tales of my dad sitting in his car outside teen discos, waiting for the last chime of music to sound. At this, he would blare his horn until they marched into his Volvo, red-faced and sullen, for their 9:30 p.m. ride home. By the time I was sixteen or seventeen, I was pretty much allowed do what I wanted, and regularly stayed out all night and into the small hours of the next day. So long as I was bright and chipper, and my school results didn't suffer, nothing was said. No doubt this was partly due to my father becoming less fearful of our independence as successive waves of his children took to their own two feet without disaster. But it's also likely that the thrill of acting as our private taxi service was beginning to dim.

Some things about having such a large family are stranger than people even think to suggest. I remember standing with my father in the kitchen of Nazareth House convent, waiting on them to deliver the truly gigantic turkey they cooked for us every Christmas. Officially, they were cooking the self-same large turkey we had brought over, since our own oven was too small to cook something big enough to feed the entire clan. But, in practice, they gave us a brand-new, much larger turkey, bearing little resemblance to our own. The turkey we were handed by Sister Angela, which had gone in the size of a ruck-sack, was now the size of a Fiat 500, resplendent in garnish and trimmings. It was the kind of thing you could imagine being taken out of the oven by a forklift, rather than a kindly nun, but that's underestimating Sister Angela, a lovely, burly woman from the west of Ireland who had a smile that could melt glass and forearms that bent steel. She was effectively Popeye in a habit, and seemed to enjoy nothing on Earth more than pre-paring us a turkey that, once eaten, we could happily strip to the bones and convert into a back bedroom.

This subterfuge was, of course, never directly acknowledged. The nuns knew my father to be a proud and dignified man, and for us to mention they'd been switching the bird every year might have made things awkward. They were soft on my dad not just because he was a lovely man who had done so much for us, but also because he donated so much of his time and effort to the community. Despite working full time as an engineer, and seeing to the upkeep, recreation and extracurricular activi-ties of his eleven children, he also served on the parish vocations council and as the school's treasurer, and was always on hand to perform any number of other duties, like recording school events on his camcorder so they could be distributed to parents.

This combined my dad's two favourite things: helping people and contriving excuses to use new technological apparatus. He took to it with the same zeal and professionalism with which he attacked all tasks. So it was that an offhand request that he record one school concert quickly snowballed into a multi-term commitment to record each nativity, musical and choir recital that ever took place while his children attended the school. For a man like my dad, this also entailed securing a rudimentary editing desk and tape-splicer, and buying multi-volume manuals on transition effects and video graphics.

My father's first camcorder came just before I was born, and made its debut at my christening in November 1985. This film is best known among our family for featuring the tail end of my dad's brief adventure with facial hair, as prolonged exposure to footage of his ill-advised moustache led him to shave it off during the editing process. By the time he was using his camcorder skills for school occasions, his efforts had progressed beyond the realm of mere recording, reflecting the swagger and dynamism that comes to a director once he's bought eighteen issues of *What Camera?* magazine and a highlighter pen. Solos are zoomed, entrances panned from one side of the stage to the other, and audience reaction shots captured with unflashy brio. My father was self-taught, but even the most discerning cineaste would have to admire the star wipes and drop-shadow WordArt title sequences, made famous by Bergman and Scorsese.

My wife has become mostly inoculated against the boredom of me breaking out this or that or another story, no longer looking for new ways to respond to the same old questioning. She can spot the subtle movements of my mouth as I wait for my turn to speak, so that I can win – win at having a big family. It's a bit like a party piece, and I've long since perfected its rhythms: get in there with the big family stuff but make sure to introduce the fact my mother died early on, since it can make people awkward if they ask about my parents and I haven't already said. Sometimes this happens with spectacular results, like when my friend Charlotte introduced me to her fabulous Swedish mother, who was particularly fascinated by the size of my family.

'Oh mi gott,' she said. 'How did your mother cope?'

'Well,' I said, with the calm, don't-worry-about-it air I've perfected for this question since my teens, 'she actually died when I was very little.'

'Cuh!' Charlotte's mum broke in with the greatest response I've ever heard. 'I'm not surprised.'

For years I've been told that my family must be such a treat to write about, since there's so much material. Well, there is, but there's also something narratively problematic about having so many people in one place at the same time. For one thing, it's hard to hold that much information in your head. Jesus had twelve apostles, and despite more than twenty years of religious instruction, services, prayer groups and sing-songs, I can name four, maybe five at most.

There's a reason Mark Twain didn't write a novel in which Huckleberry Finn, Tom Sawyer and eleven other named individuals sailed down the Mississippi on a raft. Maybe *Friends* would have been just as popular if every episode opened with eighteen pals sitting on five different couches, all speaking at once, in a dangerously overcrowded Central Perk. Perhaps, having been forced to accommodate this new, more perfect cast size, the camera would retreat back around eight feet so you could only just about make out the antics of Joey, Phoebe, Rachel, Ross, Monica, Chandler, Alan, Percy, DJ Hype, Polly, Gary A, Gary D, Stinky, Jackie, Jack, Jacquie, Boris and Claire, although you'd be surprised to discover they're all still white. No, once you start to examine storytelling dynamics, it's clear that few stirring or memorable tales are better served by tripling the number of characters in every single scene. It's often easier to focus on the real star of the show, my father, especially since I can't be bothered remembering the others' names.

5

This One Time
Daddy Lifted a Car

This one time, Daddy lifted a car. My eldest brother Dara was twelve, and had popped outside to grab his cello from the boot of the red Volvo 240 my father kept as a smaller, less mortifying vehicle when journeys didn't require a twelve-seater minibus. The boot lock was broken, so Dara thought it best to start the car, engage the electrical release switch inside, grab his preposterously large instrument and be on his way. Inevitably, the car then started to roll, sending him instantly to ground and trapping his leg in the wheel arch. Daddy heard the screams from the kitchen and ran outside to find Dara sprawled beetle-fashion on the concrete, trapped under a cello that was roughly his own size, and a Volvo now intent on breaking his leg, inch by inch. Seized by adrenalin, Daddy raced to the car and heaved at the advancing wheel arch with his bare hands, lifting 1.2 tonnes of Swedish engineering off the ground long enough for Dara to free his foot. It's a feat of strength that defies comprehension, and one my father maintains he doubtless could never have done had he not been so energised by the panic of the moment. Even Daddy was stunned by his own exertion, and the thought of what would have happened had he not managed to perform this mystifying feat of strength. But such introspection was short lived, and he was soon giving Dara, shell-shocked but miraculously unscathed, a thorough treatise on the correct use of the electronic release mechanism. 'You don't need to key the ignition,' he said as he helped Dara into the house, 'you just have to turn it to 1 to allow power from the battery to the electrics.' Dara nodded, invisible now behind the cello he was carrying on uneven feet.

This story has the air of one of those myths children tell about their dads, based on an unerring belief that their own father is the God who built the world and everything in it. I mean, it is one of those things but, conveniently, it's also something that really happened. This is proven by my father's reaction when I ask about the incident three decades later, which is to spend roughly forty seconds recounting the act of lifting an actual car off of someone, and a further eight minutes explaining how electricity is drawn from a Volvo's battery.

My father's reluctance to reflect on such achievements has been a challenge while writing this book. That's not to say that he's without conceit, of course. He is, in many ways, the most maddeningly self-assured person I know. It's just that he is a ridiculous man who takes pride in ridiculous things. He has an overweening regard for his ability to communicate with dogs, or to relate the biographical details of every single priest in Ireland. He takes great pride in recalling the licence plate of every car he's ever owned, and will dispense this list so readily it's hard not to think he occasionally practises it. He is alarmingly cocky when it comes to his skill at killing mice, a species he hates with a malevolent, black-hearted glee. It's an odd facet of his character; a man regarded by his friends as one of the kindest, gentlest humans on Earth, and by mice as Joseph Stalin. He takes particular joy in improvising weapons for the purpose, and has killed rodents with a shoe, a book and at least one bottle of holy water shaped like the Virgin Mary. He famously dispatched one with a single throw of a portable phone, without even getting out of bed. I know this because he woke us so we could inspect the furry smudge it left on his bedroom wall, before ringing my auntie in Spain to relate the entire tale.

He is much less forthcoming about the things other people praise him for, like lifting cars or battling through bereavement to raise eleven kids by himself. On this latter point, he's particularly dismissive. 'Which of you was I supposed to give back?' he replies any time we ask how he managed it, which is more often than you might think. It's a disarmingly sweet stock answer that's only slightly undercut by our usual response, which is to immediately begin suggesting suitable candidates.

Because of all these traits, his incredible strength of will and heart, and his litany of peculiar preoccupations, telling stories about Daddy – to each other, or to anyone who'll listen – is a common pastime for everyone in our family. But getting information directly from him can be tough, especially if he thinks you might use that information elsewhere, say in a book, for example. Some things he doesn't remember, others he doesn't like to talk about and still others he has actively forbidden me from mentioning. Luckily for me, and any potential reader, those things he considers too scandalous to print are usually wildly outside the range of anyone's interests but his own.

I have, alas, been sworn to secrecy on the arcane processes by which this or that cousin acquired this or that plot of land. You will not encounter within these pages even one scurrilous passage about the lengths to which my father may or may not have gone to avoid the roadworks near Castleblayney on long drives to Dublin. He makes up for these proscriptions with boundless generosity regarding material he believes *should* be included. When it comes to genealogy, dates or the names and designations of machines, townlands and priests he has known and loved, he's like the Library of Congress, and shares this information with the zeal of those people who work at Yahoo! every time someone accidentally uses their search engine. He has even, for the first time in my entire life, started calling me on the phone, to offer other information he deems relevant, should it pop into his head. 'We got the new caravan in 1990,' he'll say as I pick up the phone, my hands clammy with sweat out of fear that someone has died. Prior to this period of my life, all telecommunication with Daddy resulted from me calling him, unless it was family news like births, deaths or the arrival of an ominous-looking debt letter in any of his children's names.

'As I say, it wasn't 1989 – I found the bill of sale here. And the full length was twenty-six feet. Do you need the licence plate?'

I always match his enthusiasm, not least because I don't want him to feel like Yahoo! staff do when it inevitably transpires that their new user is just searching the word Google, but the things he deems noteworthy expand by the day. When it comes to more personal issues, or his emotional response to the trauma of our lives, it's like getting blood from a stone, but there is no upper limit to the entirely unrelated topics, phenomena or events that will prompt a cheerful 'you have to put that in the book!' He issued the directive when the actress Courteney Cox visited Derry, and is fond of ringing to describe a particularly funny political skit he's heard on local radio. He's extremely active in campaigning for the inclusion of any and all stories relating to dogs, and specifically his current dog, Sally, such as the spellbinding time she went all the way round the house and looked at him through the window. My dad is quite well read, so I can only speculate as to why the movements of dogs and priests, and detailed third-hand descriptions of Northern Irish radio comedy are deemed so essential. I have repeatedly explained that the central thesis of my book – in fact, all books that have ever been written – precludes these topics from playing a major part in a narrative, but also say that I'll see if I can fit them in.

These statements too are met with scepticism.

In a sense, my siblings and I were lucky, in that we were less inclined to take our dad for granted than other kids. We had first-hand experience of life and death, and generally doted on him. My blasé, cynical schoolfriends would have been appalled to see the glee with which we greeted him when he came home from work, or the delight we took in fussing over him on Father's Day well into our teens. But we didn't always regard him as a godlike hero, because we also had to accompany him to the shops, which was more than sufficient to ground him in our eyes. Daddy can be a difficult customer. On one occasion, he spent so long arguing with a pleasant young cashier I think my soul actually left my body. The items he was trying to buy were not, she insisted, part of the deal he was citing, and if he'd just hand over the extra £2 that was due – really not that much at all, if he thought about it – we could all be about our business. Daddy remained, both literally and figuratively, unmoved. 'The deal says three for two,' he declaimed, with the haughtiness of an archduke on the *Titanic* demanding spots on the lifeboat for him and his eight fur coats.

'That's for the smaller packs, sir,' she replied. 'If you would just read the—'

'I did read it,' he said with great exasperation, as if we were not holding up an entire shop's worth of customers, and this woman were not a cashier but a free-roaming lunatic who had entered his home and demanded he set fire to his trousers.

'I read the small print,' he repeated, 'and that's not made clear anywhere.' He had already been holding up the line for a few minutes, but it was clear he was just warming up. I think I had spotted this might happen earlier, since my dad's gaze had seemed shiftier than usual, as if he knew he might be skirting the rules a bit and was preparing for the confrontation.

There could have been another way, I'm sure. Had the cashier approached the issue with a light touch, or a note of good humour, my father could have been argued down. She was open-faced and pretty – which made this experience all the more painful for my thirteen-year-old self – but resolutely unwilling to haggle. She also hadn't realised she was standing face to face with God's one, true, perfect miser, one whose frugality was radicalised any time he felt fobbed off or ignored.

She had fallen into his trap by suggesting he hadn't read the wording on the deal when, by the time he got to the checkout, my father would know the deals of any shop as if they had been tattooed on to his skin at birth. So here we were, feeling the slow, steady tick of time trickling into an endless stalemate. My father wore the expression of a man who intends to count to six million. Tutting was audible behind us, and those shoppers who enjoyed the company of their own children began steadily decamping to other lines in the hope they might see them again before they died.

We were in West Side Stores, which had formerly been a supermarket called Crazy Prices. When I think about the evolution of Derry, I'm less likely to think of things like border checkpoints and armoured cars – both of which saw a precipitous drop in numbers during my childhood – and apt to recall places like Crazy Prices, and the shop that went there after, before it became the Quayside Tesco that stands there to this day. Crazy Prices, as its name suggests, was a shop whose branding might seem slightly, or perhaps wildly, insensitive nowadays. Its titular conceit was that the store's contents were so bafflingly discounted, so preposterously inexpensive, that they raised very real questions about the mental health of the proprietors. Their staff, and possibly their customers, were also implicated in this contagion of madness, branded throughout their locations with bulging eyes and outstretched tongues.

These prices, they implied, were so dribblesomely inscrutable that even to glance in their direction posed a very real risk of derangement. These prices weren't merely cheap, you understand, they were crazy, and any attempt to comprehend them was as pointless as considering the chasmic, gnawing depth of infinity itself. 'You must understand,' their day-glo ads seemed to say, 'if you step inside, you may never recover from these prices.' In every aisle, alongside shoulder joints for less than a pound and earthenware cooking sets for a fiver or less, it was heavily suggested you'd find people fitting and foaming at the mouth from the value of it all. To step into the produce aisle was to take your life in your hands, since you were as likely to see ten-penny apples as you were to find a random fellow customer, driven hopelessly demented by the discounts on offer, avidly shitting himself as he rolled around the floor. These were not Unreasonable Prices. Questionable Prices were not what this place was about. This was Crazy Prices, motherfucker. Grab a basket, a nappy and a straitjacket, and may God have mercy on your soul.

But this was as nothing compared to what came next. After Crazy Prices merged with Stewart's, another locally owned supermarket chain, it became West Side Stores. The name fascinated me throughout its tenure on the Strand Road, since it was never clear why it was called West Side Stores. It was known that the merger necessitated a fresh start with a new brand identity, one that didn't favour either the Stewart's or the Crazy Prices fraternity. One presumes Stewart's, who seemed as though they had a bit more sense about them, rejected portmanteaus like Batshit Stewart's or Big Stew's Mentally Ill Bargain Bin out of hand.

Whatever the case, they landed on West Side Stores, perhaps because this first store was on the western side of the city. Or maybe their numerous locations outside of Derry were all in the western part of Northern Ireland. The exact meaning was opaque, but the supermarket further muddled things by leaning into the *west* part of that name, specifically by branding each of its stores with the tropes of the American west. Everything was western-themed, from Westside Sam, their giant cowboy mascot, to the famed Cowboy Supper meal that became a local delicacy. Produce was laid out around the stores on prop barrels, and staff names were displayed on little sheriff's badges. Deals were presented with names like the 'Back to School Saddlebag Special' or the 'Honest Injun Health & Beauty Hoedown'.

It's odd to think that there must have been sober meetings about all these bizarre marketing decisions, but in any case it worked, since this baffling combination of discount retail and cowboy puns was such a hit that the store remained in Derry for five or six years. Such was its cultural impact, Tesco retained the Cowboy Supper there, and there alone, for many years afterwards. But what irked me most of all was that even if one presumed that the western branding was a vote-winner in nineties Northern Ireland, it *still* didn't make sense. West Side Stores, as I pointed out to my dad on several occasions, was clearly a pun on *West Side Story*, meaning the appropriate terrible exercise in branding that they should have gone for was that of mid-century New York, Manhattan gang wars and musical theatre.

Not that these feelings of righteous indignation were much consolation as I experienced just one of those many small-scale ego deaths that define a teenaged life.

'Now, are you going to honour the deal or not?' my father continued doggedly at the Stetson-wearing teenager who glowered across the counter.

This scenario would have been embarrassing enough, but the shopping in question, the trolley load holding up today's order of business, was a *Yee Haw What's Wrong with Your Bowels, Pardner?* hyper-multipack of toilet rolls. Plain white non-quilted toilet rolls, and in a quantity that was, as always when we bought anything in these kinds of shops, not just large but alarming. Buying toilet roll is uncomfortable at the best of times. There is always that fear, silly but present nonetheless, that my server will glance disgustedly at the paper I'm purchasing and give a look like they plan to pin my photo to a noticeboard in a back room somewhere, lining up profiles of all the disgusting people who live locally and still do shits. So standing beside a trolley that bore a precarious tower of toilet roll, so tall it dwarfed my father, myself and the steadily growing line of discontented fellow shoppers behind us, was worse still. I could feel my heart drying out and curling up inside my chest. As my father continued his dissertation on why he should be spared a two-pound surcharge for the six thousand toilet rolls he was buying, the cheapest such product available at that time outside of the former Soviet Union, I could picture in every corner of the shop an endless line of boys who were more popular, or girls I fancied, turning to see me standing there, the puny, acne-ridden progeny of this incontinent Scrooge.

Beep. The cashier rang the items through at the price my father had suggested, and he motioned for me to get them ready for transportation. She had blinked, and to anyone there who didn't know us, we must have seemed like a father-and-son team of hucksters, the kind who would have been seen pushing a cart filled with scrap through dustbowl-era Kansas but who, in Derry, were reduced to selling their ill-gotten gains on the lucrative black market for discount toilet paper.

*

These kinds of experiences were a staple of my childhood, and fixed for me the image of my father as a miser, particularly when he would later instruct us on the usage of that very shipment of toilet paper. It was his contention, argued many times and at least once at the dinner table, that one sheet, judiciously used, was sufficient for most movements – I believe he even mimed specific foldings that could be employed in helping us achieve this feat. So, to some extent, this reputation was earned. He also never bought branded cereals or snacks; we feasted instead on those supermarket variants that were almost but not quite like the target brand. 'Wow,' we'd say, in between diffident bites of our Puffin bars, 'Tesco must have really good lawyers.' But this perception of him was massively unfair, since he worked extremely hard and earned a good wage by Derry standards, and spent all of it trying to manage an unreasonably large household. It's striking how little I understood this at the time, which was a direct consequence of all the measures he took to make sure we never felt poorer than anyone else.

Considering he spent his adult life giving the staff at the Northern Irish Birth Registry premature arthritis, it's surprising that my father was himself an only child. His mother's name was Mary, and his father was a carpenter named Joseph (I know), and they lived in Belleek, County Fermanagh. My paternal grandfather died before I was born, and Granny O'Reilly when I was just two, after spending her final months in our family home. As a schoolmistress, Granny O'Reilly was a pillar of the community in Belleek, and my father tells stories of local men lining up to have their forms, applications or legal documents looked over and signed by her at a time when illiteracy was widespread.

The few photographs I possess of Granny O'Reilly show she was hard to age. It sometimes seems as though all Irish people from the past were born old and then proceeded to age like the pears you get in an all-night garage, accumulating freckles, liver spots and clicking noises at the bendy parts, achieving their final form by around the age of thirty-five. There are photos of my dad when he was seventeen and he already looks like a full-grown man. I'm thirty-five and dress like a toddler. When my father was a teenager, he looked as though he already had a pet name for his favourite stepladder. For older generations, this effect was even more pronounced. The photographic record shows that Granny O'Reilly began her life aged sixty-eight and proceeded to grow smaller and older from there. There are pictures of her with my father as a very small child, which logic dictates must place her in her thirties, and yet her wild hair and deadening glare present the steely mien of a woman many decades her senior. She was stern-faced with a shock of white hair and thick, scowl-prone eyebrows, which made her look like the sort of person who'd keep her arms folded on a trampoline. She was also my dad's teacher throughout his primary education, a situation I don't believe thrilled my shy and retiring father, and which added a certain frisson to the much-feared faux pas of calling your teacher Mum. In what seems like a cruel trap, any time he did accidentally make this fairly understandable lapse, he was upbraided for it in front of the whole class. By his actual mum.

*

Daddy might have been, by instinct, a more stoical, less effusive father, which makes not just his parenting but the love with which he undertook it all the more impressive. He had a lot on his plate, so maybe it's OK that he occasionally held up supermarkets with toilet roll purchases.

He is almost comically square, and has more odd ideas about the ways of the world than I can fit in one book. Focusing on, say, that time he had a row with my brother for bumping into him while they were riding dodgem cars – coining the memorable exclamation 'They're called dodgems, not crashems!' – allows us to humanise him for ourselves and others. The fact that my father's ideal bumper-car experience is one in which dozens of stone-faced children carefully evade each other in total silence can surely only add to the esteem in which he is regarded. Slack-jawed awe is the default reaction I get when I talk about my dad and what he did for us, and rightly so, but my dad hates this kind of sentimentality – and its close cousin, pity – more than he hates traffic wardens, or broccoli. Luckily, he has a ready stock of foibles ripe for us to tease him about. Like all older Irish men, he marries a high-minded rejection of all things modern with a near-chronic addiction to trash culture. My father will roll his eyes when I say 'cool', as if lingo that bleedingly hip is an insult to the martyred poets of Ireland, and yet five minutes later will tell me that Nick Knowles has gone country, and the new steel guitar album he debuted on *Loose Women* sounds a marked improvement on his last.

He knows, vaguely, what a high-five is, but his handle on the concept is so loose he once announced one with a tender, hopeful cry of 'slap my hand high up in the air', a declaration that has become something of a family motto. The Christmas before last, he announced, and demonstrated, his total ignorance of rock, paper, scissors, as either a term or concept, and subsequently refused to believe it was a known thing. He has a similar reluctance to accept the existence of the Easter Bunny, which he claims was only invented in the last few years. Stranger still, of course, are those phenomena that do not exist, but which he believes in with every fibre of his being. My father holds horses to be malevolent, because one stood on his foot when he was a boy – this despite living near horses for most of his life, not least the rotating cast of ponies that have been put to pasture in the field directly behind our house. He choked on a fishbone when he was quite small, and the experience so scarred him that we were all told fish was an incredibly dangerous foodstuff and should be eaten only in fillet, finger or nugget form, if at all. To serve someone fish with any or all of its skeleton intact is, to my father, roughly equivalent to feeding someone the contents of a Hoover bag.

Sometimes my father's eccentricities bend the world around him, conforming to the strangeness of his own mind, as when he became irate at a slow driver on the motorway and kept calling him a clown, only to overtake him and find that the driver was indeed a man in full clown make-up. And then there are his passions. My father's idea of heaven is to stand in the aisles of a hardware store with a list of impossibly fiddly screws to gather, preferably so disparately spaced he can survey the entire shop's contents for eternity. Throughout my childhood, any trip out of the house would usually feature an unjustifiable detour to a B&Q or garden centre, from which he would emerge with six hundred glow-in-the-dark cable ties, a box of satirical gnomes and enough random pig iron to keep his available stock of nuts and bolts hovering at an even two hundred thousand.

At my age, my father had five children and lived in a home he had surveyed, designed and built from scratch himself. I pay half my wage to live in a Hackney breadbin and feel like Bear Grylls when I sharpen a pencil with a knife. My dad drafted, constructed and installed septic tanks for his own homes, and for water treatment facilities all over Northern Ireland. If my sink were to get blocked right now, I would call the police. But beside all this, possibly the greatest achievement of my father's parenting was letting us know that we were loved, and moreover giving us the knowledge that to love – and be loved – was the most important of things. This at a time when most of the men we knew couldn't have found the will or way to express their feelings if their lives depended on it. Looking back, some of their lives literally did. I've always felt that we, his horrible, mocking children, take so much joy from making fun of him, telling tales of miserly standoffs in supermarkets, or overly zealous lectures on toilet roll application, because it punctures the worshipful regard in which we hold him, and brings him down to our level. But we love him to the end of the world and back, and thankfully possess the ease with that love to tell him all the time, in between mercilessly teasing him.

Now, we mostly live away, and Father's Day is spent sending him WhatsApp videos from the grandkids and calling him to see if he liked the jumper/socks/Irish country CD we've sent him. But when we were children, he awoke each Father's Day to the sound of soft padding at the carpet outside his room, and the doorknob stiffly turning as we filed in, conveying good wishes for the holiday. Or, more likely, he would have woken one hour earlier, to small, quick feet scurrying through the hall and to the kitchen, where his special breakfast was prepared. In that thick way of children, we had mastered the art of whispering louder than we spoke, and a cacophony of hushed screams, frantic scribbling and clanging saucepans would resound through the house, masked only by the steady clatter of moderately serious trips and falls, themselves so common as to have become white noise.

I imagine my father sat up in bed with a book set aside for the purpose, studiously ignoring the fights breaking out among the grubby little servers now traipsing down the hall, pushing a battered tea trolley towards his door. This contraption was three turns of a screw away from being shrapnel, and sported thick brass wheels which, even on the plush brown carpet of our hall, made a noise like the Eiffel Tower being folded into a quarry. It would groan under the weight of a cooked breakfast, some inane trinkets, a flower, an errant sock and the multi-coloured foliage of our many crumpled handmade cards. Once we'd made our way down the hall with all the stately grace of an exploding foal, my father's bedroom door was thrown open. Feigning alarm and surprise, he pretended he'd only just now been roused by the eleven children unloading on to his carpet, pyjama-striped and laughing, like the freckled contents of a rural Irish clown car.

Standing in that bedroom, we'd laugh as he delighted over his plate of burned rashers, runny eggs and beans that looked like they'd been pre-digested. Luckily for him, we'd interrupt this feast to thrust our cards in his face. We would sing songs and read poems and hand him gifts; one year I gave him a frankly terrifying sculpture of him that I'd constructed from pasta shells. Back then I knew how to sum up what he meant to me. Thirty years later I'm content to reach for that, even if he'd probably prefer I wrote an entire chapter about dogs and priests.

6

An Entire Chapter About Dogs and Priests

Father Huck Balance stood in full vestments, scowling at the dog as the wind wrapped his stole around his face. He had been swinging the thurible fairly hard, and milky incense was now spewing out of it in a dense, Catholic fog. Rain was beginning to fall, and the smell of ozone mingled with the sweet musk of Mass to create an uncanny feeling of everything being out of place. It was the kind of grey, half-started day you're always reading about in Irish short stories, where strong, unreasonable men attend the rural funerals of even stronger and less reasonable men. This was weather fit for killing your uncle, or nearly-but-not-quite bringing the wake house to a standstill by confessing your love for the widow of the departed, a woman you haven't seen since that last time, so many years ago, that you, our author, are certainly about to describe in some detail. But we were not gathered by a hillside

grave, nor huddling toward a country wake. We were standing outside our house waiting for the priest to bless our new
twenty-six-foot ABI Award Superstar caravan. It was July 1992,
just nine months after my mother's death. By this point, I was
likely so inured to Catholic rituals – and my family's common
deployment of them – that events like this, though interesting,
even exciting, didn't seem particularly odd. I've since realised
that most families did not have priests out to the house to bless
their caravan; it was more the sort of thing that bishops would
do at Dublin airport with the plane carrying the Irish football
team to a major tournament.

Even for a family like ours, who were fairly used to priests
calling round, seeing one in full regalia, just walking around
our house and garden, was a thrill. It was a cousin of that confusion you get when you spot a teacher in the supermarket.
Here the feeling was multiplied, since Father Balance arriving
in his full rig produced the opposite effect of a teacher sighted
in the wild. Outside of school, teachers could seem pathetic
and drab, shorn of the power that hung about them in their
natural habitat. I once saw Mr Johnston in West Side Stores. A
man who breathed fire and crushed souls from 8 until 3 each
day, now pondering, dead-eyed, whether to buy a 3-for-2 pack
of Rootin' Tootin' Cottage Pies, or a shop-soiled Vegetable
Varmint Vegan Lasagne. Father Huck, by contrast, brought
the magnificence of his station with him, as if Christ's power
was not just all-encompassing but conveniently portable. On
secondment to this outpost, he transplanted the gravitas of his
own, greater universe to the spot between our house and the
garage, projecting it entirely on to the large caravan in front
of him. As we pulled our sleeves down over our hands against

the cold, he stood implacable and resolute, broadcasting the solemnity of God in the very same place where, just twenty-five minutes earlier, our dog, Nollaig, had been eating his own shite.

Nollaig was no longer ingesting effluent, but still refused to honour that half-state of reverence the rest of us were attempting, the type of quiet awkwardness that's general when you have Mass in a weird place and everyone tries to act as though it's perfectly normal. He was barking and growling, as if mocking the events unfolding in front of him. Father Balance said nothing, but I thought I caught a glint of contempt in his eyes at each interruption. What, he seemed to say to our dog, is so funny about a priest blessing a gigantic caravan in the rain? I presume the smell of the incense was what was bothering Nollaig. Either that or Mr Devenney, our otherwise kindly neighbour, had landed us with one of Ireland's few Protestant sheepdogs. Such dogs could, of course, sow discord among the others, annex the lands of Catholic cows and march provocatively past contested field routes each July. On the plus side, most farmers agreed, Protestant dogs would probably be more willing to put in a shift on Sundays.

Whatever his denomination, Nollaig – Christmas in Irish – had long established a reputation as something of a cheerful arsehole, and was less a beloved pet than an uncaring brute who tumbled through our lives like a demented frat boy in an American campus comedy. We all pretended we liked him, perhaps out of fear he'd steal our lunch money or push us into a drinking fountain. He'd been a gift for my sister Mairead the year before my mother died, although a combination of his spirited nature and Mairead's being just seven led to her slowly being forgiven of prime responsibility, and it was instead assumed that he was the family's problem. He ate everything he could get his paws on, and several things he should never have been able to. He once savaged a frozen chicken that had been in one of the two big chest freezers we had in the garage. How he managed to open its lid, which was large, heavy and stood four feet off the ground, is still a matter of speculation. When Conall was two years old he grabbed Nollaig's lead in a fit of misplaced affection, and Nollaig shot off at such speed that the baby of the family was jolted, Buster Keaton fashion, off the ground. For a few seconds he trailed behind our dyspeptic hound in mid-air, fully horizontal, as his little fist gripped the tether now hurtling him toward certain death. In the end, Conall got away with a few cuts and bruises, but for him, my parents and most of the rest of my family, it was extraordinarily traumatic. Personally, I consider it one of the best things I've ever seen, and feel as though it made the rest of Nollaig's bad behaviour broadly worth it. In any case, whatever his thoughts on virgin births or the holy catechism, there was just as much a chance Nollaig was dismissive of priests due to general misanthropy rather than outright sectarianism. In the end, I'm happy to presume our dog was a prick, not a bigot.

Pursued by Nollaig, Father Balance raised his hands and approached the caravan with grave intent. Birds squawked and gravel crunched underfoot as he stepped forward to mutter a blessing. He swung the thurible around the wheels and then the windows, and then round the back, as if there was a preset routine for such things, an off-the-peg setting for a caravan blessing that was second nature to any priest. Within a few minutes the deed was done, and we dispersed in the joyful knowledge that some small part of God's portable power was now embedded in our caravan.

Such were the perks of knowing so many priests. When I was a child, it seemed as though my dad knew every priest in Ireland. This is because he knew every single priest in Ireland. Irish priests happen to be my father's specialist subject. By this, I do not mean the Irish priesthood, as in the history and customs of that institution (though on that topic, too, he is undeniably strong). I mean the literal, individual priests. Each of them. By name, location and family connection. Ireland's small population, combined with my parents' energetically devout Catholicism, put them on friendly terms with most of Ireland's clergy during that extensive period of the twentieth century when Ireland was a net exporter of priests.

It's worth explaining just how comically, parodically Catholic my parents were. They weren't just avid churchgoers and committed in their home lives, they also gave readings at Mass and served as eucharistic ministers, handing out communion to parishioners. They worked within various Catholic-flavoured remits: charities, prayer groups and councils that gave a papist slant on marriage, vocation and youth outreach. My mother spent her entire professional career teaching in Catholic secondary schools, and my father volunteered as treasurer of our Catholic primary. More memorably still, there was a short period in the late nineties when he taught computer skills to the nuns who lived in the attached convent. We more than once visited Catholic sites like Lourdes and Knock on family holidays and experienced the true scalding heat of boredom at large, outdoor Masses in the wind and rain of holy fields. Before I was born, my parents took the opportunity to embark on a cross-continental trip that took in not Florence and the Louvre, Barcelona or the Algarve, but the many and splendid Marian shrines of Europe.

There was also, let's be honest, the fact that they had eleven cardigan-wearing little children, arguably the most solid credential that exists within Catholicism short of holy orders. They were paragons of piety, and aspired to raise the lower-middle-class ideal of a good Catholic family. If only one of us had managed to spot a statue of the Virgin Mary riding a bike or smoking a fag, it's a fair bet my mother would be a saint by now. Unfortunately, after the golden years of the early twentieth century, during which it seemed that barely a week went past without such a sighting, the boom was over by our time, strangely coinciding with the advent of reliable compact photography.

It's sometimes hard for me to work out whether we were ourselves especially holy, or if we simply lived through a particularly holy time for my mother, when her faith gained greater expression in the face of death. I was well into adulthood before I realised that in every single memory I have of my mother, she was living with cancer, or the fear of its recurrence. But while it does seem that her faith was strengthened by her illness, it's also true that she was very committed to begin with. The Catholicism of my parents leaned less on dogma and more on a generalised sense of gratitude, humility and fellowship, and an emphasis on family and community. They didn't go for diatribes about hell, sin, masturbation and abortion. We did hear about that stuff in school and at Mass – most especially abortion, which was almost always described as part of 'the culture of death', to use the church's favourite phrase of the time – but even then only infrequently.

Insofar as evil was ever mentioned to me as a child, it was less in relation to touching myself or fancying boys and more to do with present, quotidian sins, like making fun of people with disabilities or becoming involved in paramilitary violence. On this latter point, my parents were particularly clear. Contrary to the narrative often pushed by outside chroniclers of the Troubles, the sectarianism we saw everywhere growing up was not so much religious as tribal. In Derry, a Catholic didn't mean someone who had internalised the virgin birth and the transubstantiation of Christ's corpse into a sliver of cheap, waxy, haunted wafer. *Catholic* in the common parlance merely meant someone who was born of Catholics, no matter what their feelings about Christ's literal existence, or their opinion on the Second Vatican Council. The Catholics who made up the IRA were almost exclusively Catholics in this sense, and the same was true of all the Catholics mentioned on the news after each round of murders. They were Catholics in that they were not Protestants, and vice versa. My parents, on the other hand, were Catholics in the more full-strength prescription of the term, and lived the values of tolerance, kindness, mercy and forgiveness that perhaps organised Catholicism didn't represent at the time.

The local farmers were less forgiving of Nollaig than we were when he graduated from mauling frozen chickens to killing and eating their sheep. It shouldn't have been surprising, perhaps, since he had for a while been growing more bold, nipping at visitors and issuing growls and even bites that had long since progressed beyond playful. One cold, wet Sunday – again adding fuel to the whole Protestant theory – Nollaig killed a sheep a few fields over and was put down. I don't believe a vet was involved; it was instead agreed that Nollaig should be presented to the farmer himself, so that he could have a full, frank conversation via shotgun. We weren't exactly distraught, but our neighbours threw street parties. We suddenly had that disquieting realisation that everyone within an eight-mile radius had hated him as much as they loved us. I guess it was the dog-owner's equivalent of when your friend breaks up with her boyfriend and everyone finally tells her that his beard is disgusting and that podcast of his is going nowhere.

Perhaps inevitably, we entered into a rebound relationship, taking in an Alsatian/Labrador cross named Bruno, who was everything Nollaig hadn't been. Bruno was a girl who we initially thought was a boy, hence her name. We twigged she was a girl when it became clear she was pregnant. It seemed as though she had come from nowhere, but now I wonder if she had been a stray notch on Nollaig's bedpost who, after keeping as far away from her psycho ex as possible, swooped in and nicked his bed once he was out of the picture. She was quiet and kind-hearted and immediately proved more popular than poor Nollaig, but often flinched from contact, especially from men, which made us think she'd had a troubled time of it. Desperate to love and be loved, I saw in her a kindred spirit, and doted on her unreservedly. Since my mother's death, we each sought the opportunity to project our neuroses onto the family pet, and here was one that finally seemed aware of our presence. For those of us suffering a lack of attention, we adored her steadfast fascination with everything we did. For those of us who wanted space, we had a little underling we could chase from any rooms we entered, with an alacrity that suggested we might want to do the same to some of the house's human occupants.

I think I just wanted someone I could repeatedly express my love for, without having to think too much about why, exactly, I needed it so much. I should be clear, this wasn't *Bleak House*; my family were open about how much we loved each other, and my father especially. It's just he probably would have been freaked out if I'd said it four hundred times a day which is, approximately, what I needed to do at the time. An oddly co-dependent little friendship was forged. I cared for Bruno by treating her very kindly, and she cared for me by not taking off. Two pitiful little eejits, each sad in their own way. I performed those tasks a motherless child might imagine a mother would do: walking beside my furry little infant, saying 'I love you' and 'I'll never leave you' and 'do not eat that dead bird, it's been at the side of the road for two weeks'.

When her litter finally arrived, these instincts went into overdrive, and I looked on each of her offspring as my personal responsibility. Like some little Irish Oedipus, I mapped new frontiers of dysfunction by casting myself as Bruno's mother, son and, now, proud father to her eleven pups. While they were little more than squirming, wriggling caterpillars, too small to open their eyes, us Wee Ones handballed them to and fro, sizing them up and allotting each an equal sequence of cuddles and pattings, courting near constant admonition from my father that we treat them a little more gently. Had he not been on hand, I fear more than a few would have been squeezed to death. It was clear we were not especially attuned to the finer points of animal husbandry, as we discovered one particularly hot day when Conall became flustered at the thought of them growing parched, unspooled the hose by our garage and directed a torrent of water directly into the kennel to 'cool them down'. The next thing we knew, he'd sent a squadron of bemused little pups sailing on a river of soaked bedding, hay and hundreds of their tic-tac sized turds. But they survived, and soon their eyes were open and they were yapping and squealing like actual little dogs, and producing copious amounts of larger, more substantial, shite.

Three weeks in, I was woken by a distant whine, and followed the pups' mewling cries to the top of the road. It was just before dawn, and raining hard. I found them huddled beneath a shipping container by the customs checkpoint, and climbed under to inspect them. There was more than enough space for me to sit there cross-legged, and as I did, they gambolled into my lap, their drenched bodies patting me all at once like a sad applause of frightened little hands. There was no sign of their mother, although I could hear her barking in the very same field of sheep that had done for Nollaig. I sat there in the full horror of their abandonment, holding these soaked pups and crying. Daddy was soon alerted to my absence and a little while later he arrived for me, sending Dara and Shane back for a towel to grab the litter. He told me Bruno's instructive instinct had kicked in and she'd likely brought the pups up there to hunt sheep, but finding they preferred to flop around uselessly in the rain went on without them. Sister Annette took me out of class the following day to tell me, in the curious terminology used in such cases, that Bruno had been 'worrying sheep' and 'had had to be destroyed'. Even as a child, the idea that chasing sheep 'worried' them seemed preposterous, conjuring images of flocks pacing back and forth, of flighty ewes biting their nails. And as for 'destroyed', I didn't even know where to start with that one. They were talking about Bruno as if she were an asteroid hurtling toward Earth, or a nuclear warhead. I imagined piles of bold dogs, stacked like a cache of decommissioned paramilitary ordnance. I've since been told this isn't too far off the truth.

I wonder now why they had to tell us at all, but then I suppose, unlike with my city friends, they couldn't pretend she'd gone to live on a farm. Perhaps they could have reversed it and told me she had been sent to live in a council high-rise in town, but that apparently never occurred to them. Our neighbours didn't throw parties this time, and even the farmer who was forced to report her gave his condolences to my father, since he knew it would be a heavy blow. I was inconsolable for weeks, and it doesn't take a particularly deep grasp of psychology to work out what I saw in these eleven helpless infants, senselessly deprived of a mother. It was pretty heavy-handed stuff but, what can I say, God's a bit of a hack sometimes.

While my parents would not have agreed with that statement, their Catholicism was less dogmatic and more a happy-clappy Christian fellowship-type thing; all summer camps and trendy books written by cool priests with nice hair. Not that we were too outwardly zealous. We'd see Americans on TV crying in church or speaking in tongues and reflect that even the most ardent Catholics we knew were more likely to mumble their way through the rosary. That kind of ostentatious religion just didn't seem to suit Northern Irish Catholics. American evangelicals seemed to treat God as their best friend, and American Catholics in Irish and Italian gangster movies treated him as a reclusive weirdo who had an ungovernable obsession with their genitals. Catholics of the English upper classes, like Evelyn Waugh and Graham Greene, were even weirder, obsessed with blood and candles, and appearing to think of their godhead as an occult dominatrix who issued pellets of shame and guilt like a giant, sadomasochistic Pez dispenser. That wasn't how most Northern Irish Catholics would have framed it. God was a boring but avuncular boss, or a more senior friend from work, someone to whom you'd be polite if you bumped into them down the shops, but most certainly not one you'd wish to spend time with outside office hours. Our version of carefree papism was the kind where everyone stuck their heads down for the prayers and said very little, but occasionally a laughing priest might tell you about a recent go he'd had on a bouncy castle and how, in a funny kind of a way, isn't our Lord Jesus a bit like a bouncy castle, when you think about it?

We went to Mass every Sunday without fail, and did confession, communion and confirmation, but everyone did that. My second week at college was actually the first time I'd ever gone two weeks in a row without attending Mass. I never went regularly again. I had been more involved with the church than most of the kids in the parish, since our family did the readings every few weeks, and as more of us went off to university the pool of available readers was winnowed to those of us who were left, so we'd each end up doing four or five a year. Giving the readings did manage to eradicate any embarrassment I had about public speaking, which was useful in later life. I had used all that embarrassment up by the age of thirteen, which was the last time I used the stool that was placed by the lectern for smaller speakers. Having misjudged the effects of a recent growth spurt, I ascended the stool to discover I was now fully three feet above the microphone and my gangly frame and arched back gave me the look of a professional basketball player bobbing for apples. Mortified, I ignored the laughter – the loudest of which was coming from my own siblings – and gave both readings as the world's tallest man, refusing to climb down even as I stood in silence while the Hallelujah was sung from the back of the church.

Sometimes Daddy would come home from meetings on youth engagement or vocations outreach, re-energised by the mission of getting kids to love the church, and use us as an impromptu little focus group he could bounce ideas off. Sitting at the dinner table, he'd affect a ponderous air and wrestle with the task of making young people think Christ was 'cool'. Should Father Bun Hanratty mention Oasis more in his sermons, perhaps? Maybe the church could pretend that Jesus Christ was the mysterious one in a boy band or – now squinting at some notes written in scrawly fountain pen – lived in Planet Hollywood. Would we like that? Would we like it if Jesus Christ wore a leather jacket and lived in Planet Hollywood? Because if we did, it was suggested, my dad could make that happen.

Some priests knew us so well they would drop by unannounced, as when Father McKenna and Father McLaughlin took a jaunt out to the country on a whim and sidled up to our house on bicycles. Ireland has spent the past thirty years shedding its attachment to the Catholic church faster than any other country in Europe, but even if we continued to secularise for a century or more, we would likely still agree that it's always nice to see a priest on a bicycle. There is just something pleasing, something primal, iconic and utterly silly about the image. Possibly only a tandem could have bettered it, perhaps decorated with stickers of favourite saints.

On other occasions, a priest's arrival could be more surprising, as when we returned home from an all-day trip to visit Auntie Kathleen in South Armagh and found Father Finbar Staples sitting in the living room watching *Match of the Day*. He had arrived earlier that afternoon and, upon discovering we were out, jimmied open our kitchen window and made himself at home until we returned, several hours later. What's truly astonishing is not the event itself, but how muted our response to it was. At the time, it didn't seem all that strange that he'd done this, certainly not to my dad, who was just happy to see an old friend, and even apologised that there wasn't much to eat in the house. We were dispatched to make tea and cut up some fruitcake for the poor Father, who was likely wasting away on the meagre rations of crisps, biscuits, a ham sandwich, a jar of olives and three beers he'd had to make do with in our absence. For his part, Father Finbar didn't seem even remotely embarrassed by any of this, and happily threw himself into a catch-up with my father – a man whom, prior to breaking into his home, he hadn't seen in three or four years. When it came time for Father Finbar to take off, my father apologised again, as if it was poor form of us to have been absent, or at the very least not to have had the house fully stocked with priestly provisions. It was as if once you were baptised Catholic, you tacitly understood that your home was a waystation for any passing priest and the houses of rural Ireland were a tasty network of clerical birdfeeders. My dad still isn't really sure why we find this story so funny, save for the final verdict it provided on Elmo's qualities as a guard dog. Upon discovering a man in black was fumbling with our kitchen window, Father Finbar maintained she had done nothing more than lick his hand and nudge his forearm.

Elmo was Bruno's daughter, and probably the best dog we ever had. She combined Bruno's quiet temperament with a more outgoing personality and, her abilities as a watchdog notwithstanding, a keen intelligence. My father was particularly strident when it came to championing her IQ, and he quickly established a working theory on her failure to stop our clerical intruder. Elmo could, so my father insisted, intuit that Father Finbar was a friendly figure, but if he had been someone with malign intent she would have dealt with him differently. As always, when it comes to my dad's theories of canine intelligence – for they are many and varied – no real detail was forthcoming on exactly what Elmo would have done in this circumstance. Called the police, perhaps. Such was the power of Elmo's personality that even her failings were repurposed into strengths, and such was her charisma that we all went along with it.

Elmo had a grace and poise that conferred a certain nobility on her, even in youth. She lacked the impulsivity or recklessness of other dogs, as if she was in possession of information beyond their reach, giving her an inner well of confidence that stopped her from over-reacting to things. She was sincerely empathetic, and had a dozen quiet gestures of comfort she could deploy if you needed emotional support. Elmo showed my father's softer side, since there's no greater love than that between a taciturn rural Irishman and the dog he shouts at all day. The attachment between them was immediate, and long lasting. When I remember her, it's at my father's side as he undertook some task in his office; sitting sphinx-like behind the garage, watching the world go by on the main road; or snoozing on that same patch under the kitchen table where the lino sits directly over pleasingly heated pipes. As my father settled into middle age, Elmo was the ideal companion: affectionate enough that her company made him feel loved and appreciated, but sufficiently independent she didn't really require any actual looking after.

Compared to Bruno, who had been a total homebody, Elmo was like a chirpy, self-assured little foreign exchange student. She spent most of her time ranging through the Derry/Donegal countryside, often returning to the house only for mealtimes and naps. One time she was spotted about five miles away on the Craigavon bridge, close to Derry's city centre. On other occasions she would be dropped back in nice family cars by friendly strangers, who hadn't just encountered her randomly but, it usually turned out, had built a relationship with her over some weeks or even months. Their children, clearly besotted, would refer to her with unfamiliar names, evincing some form of ownership over this wise and friendly dog that, unbeknownst to them, had been gaming the entire county for food. Her travels hadn't merely been a whistle-stop tour through the borderlands' scenic spots, but to any family home without a dog in a four- or five-mile radius of our house. I'm not sure how many families were involved, but it's a good thing she covered so much ground as she had four or five dinners to burn off every day.

Elmo was also the first experience I had of my father's remarkable animal telepathy skills, which he retains to this day. 'She understands every word you say, you know,' he was fond of telling us. They lived in complete harmony with each other. Elmo shared my father's frustration at nuisance callers pulling into our drive with requests to buy the caravan or in the hope of persuading Daddy to become a Jehovah's Witness. And Daddy was firmly in her corner when it came to her ongoing feud with the swallows that nested in our garage, and who took cruel delight in dipping over her with sarcastic swooping motions. While my father read nothing but good intentions into the minds of dogs, he clearly didn't like what his avian mind-sensors picked up, and found that birds were, for the most part, obnoxious twats. 'They know what they're doing!' he'd say, incensed, as they darted back and forth above her kennel like a malignant little squadron of Red Arrows.

We discovered that Elmo's travels were not quite as PG-rated as we presumed when she had pups of her own, fathered by some unknown, distant Lothario. We gave away all but one, Sophie, in whom she delighted, teaching her to hunt by chasing not sheep but the ever-circling swallows, which were much closer and proved less hazardous prey. All looked to be going well until Sophie was a month or two old, at which point she contracted pneumonia and became gravely ill. She died on Christmas Eve, leaving us despondent and, we thought, removing some small bit of Elmo's sunny demeanour for ever.

Priests died too. 'Ach no,' Daddy would say, ruffling the pages of the *Derry Journal* for effect as he spoke to no one in particular. 'There's Hustings LeFarge dead anyway.' As with his love for

Formula One, I often thought he was disappointed we didn't share his fascination with church goings-on. We weren't rendered dizzily incontinent by the inside track he had regarding clerical matters: who was going to a new parish, who had a new car, who'd been on the radio and who'd died – *especially* who'd died. Following a silence, or perhaps some mumbled words of sympathy, Daddy would expound on Father LeFarge, recounting his many-staged career with mounting astonishment that none of his own infant children were better acquainted with that time he baptised six babies that had fallen in a hedge, or spread awareness of Passion Sunday by touring the country with a kissing booth. It's a true strength of my father's parenting style that he always spoke to us as though we were adults, ignoring the difference in age between us and himself. However, a curious side effect of this was his tendency to grow incredulous that we were not adults and didn't have the experience or memories he had accrued over his own lifetime. We would have to keep insisting that we knew little about the career of a ninety-year-old priest he'd last seen a few decades before we were born. 'Where was it he was prelate?' Daddy might then muse, addressing this query to a room of children who'd barely been out of the house, much less knew the movements of an elderly Jesuit from Sligo.

We had an anniversary Mass in our house every year for my mother, and friends and family would come to commemorate her passing with a relatively informal service in our sitting room. It was a bit mad seeing the sofa and armchairs replaced with rows of folding chairs we'd borrow from our primary school. The ordinary running order of a Mass would be broken up with more personal touches: people sharing memories or stories, and funny, tear-jerking little films made by my dad showing old photos or camcorder footage he'd put together. These videos were the highlight, done with a care and wit that was as apt to make the room burst into laughter as tears. They also gave me the only experience I can remember of seeing my mother moving through life in anything like a normal way, of her laughing or scowling at my dad for filming her, of her saying my name out loud. The work he'd pour into them was evident in every frame, and showed not just his love for Mammy, and for us, but his love of making that love known. Never particularly solemn in the early days, after a few years these occasions became openly joyous experiences, celebrations of her life and a lovely time for the family to return to the house and be together, no matter where fortune had sprayed them across the map.

The Masses were said by Father Bun McAliskey, the priest who baptised me and oversaw my communion, confirmation and each weekly Mass. We continued to do these Masses for twenty years, until Father McAliskey did our service, said his goodbyes and stood up in church the following morning to announce he was leaving the priesthood. He received rapturous applause and the full support of the congregation, ours included; we were slack-jawed and touched by the fact he'd obviously kept my mother's Mass as his last appointment in religious orders.

By then, Elmo's youthful demeanour had given way to a more mature and stately poise. The grey in her muzzle transformed that youthful nobility into something like gravitas and, in the manner of an actress making do with the paucity of good

Hollywood roles, she made an overnight transition from ingénue to wise old priestess. It was clear her joints were bothering her, and a rheumy film gathered in her eye that looked decidedly suboptimal. She was soon chasing birds that simply were not there. On one fateful run in 2004, a car came in bearing the news we'd feared. She'd been identified, unmoving, on the road. My dad retrieved the body and, devastated, buried her in a plot behind the garage, overlooking the field in which she spent so much of her time, with a pleasant view of the road and happily off the path of those tormenting, tumbling birds.

My father took over presenting duties the following year, since replacing a priest seemed, by that stage, as blasphemous as swapping out his beloved dog. That year the occasion was pitched as an evening of commemoration. It would be the last such service we did.

Something my dad reminds me of when we talk of my lapsed faith is that the church's worst ideas don't indict all Catholics. This is a sentiment with which I wholeheartedly agree, since in my experience ordinary rank-and-file Catholics are mostly decent and lovely people, who don't literally agree with every little church teaching. But with Catholicism, you are in or you are out. You don't get to pick and choose the bits you agree with, by definition. It's like saying you're a teetotaller who only drinks wine. There was once a huge movement toward creating a subset of Catholics who 'agree with Catholicism except this bit or that bit' and it became wildly popular with the public. It was called the Reformation, and those people are called Protestants.

A year after Elmo died, we forced another dog onto Daddy without really giving him much say in the matter, since we knew he'd say he didn't want one. Luckily, it proved a massive and immediate success. The Labrador/retriever cross who has lived with him for the past ten years is, by some distance, his favourite child. From the gloom of loss, a bright shining star entered his orbit, and Daddy didn't so much form a bond with her as initiate a cult in her name. Sally sends him birthday cards, ghost-written by my sister Caoimhe, which dwarf our own when they're propped above the fireplace, crowding out the view like a ship's sail he's placed on the mantelpiece.

I think it's fair to say that Sally isn't quite as noble, wise or clever as Elmo. I got myself in a lot of trouble by claiming in a newspaper column that she lacked the intelligence God gave a sea sponge. Within minutes I was being sent images of the dog reading the *Observer*, with what I'm sure my father hoped I'd see as an upset expression. Unfortunately, Sally lacks the capacity to look anything other than delighted when she's in my father's company, so the effect was slightly undone. What Sally lacks in poise and grace she more than makes up for in being huge, hairy and filled with adoration. 'To his dog,' wrote Aldous Huxley, 'every man is Napoleon; hence the popularity of dogs.' Napoleon would be a sad demotion for my father, as Sally believes him to be God himself. And for all his religious devotion, my father is fine with that.

7

Fermanagh

'These are all the ones I have,' Patricia says, handing over a tightly wrapped bundle of envelopes. We're speaking at a family get-together, to which she has been invited as my mother's oldest friend. She'd heard I was writing a book, because my dad's first response to the news that I was writing a book was to tell every person he's ever met that I was writing a book. Soon, I was getting Facebook messages from old friends like Patricia, and also from people I didn't quite know but whose profile pictures were either a freeze-frame of them trying to grapple with their webcam, or a close-up from a wedding, zoomed in to the point that their entire face was about four pixels wide.

'Daddy,' I said on one such occasion, 'did you tell Miss Graumann I was writing a book?'

'I did,' he replied, in his best thank-me-later drawl. 'I ran into her in Lidl. She was very pleased, you know: she always thought you were great at English.'

'She was my German teacher, Daddy – that's not even a compliment. Who else have you told?'

'Oh, the silver surfers WhatsApp group, Kieran at the pharmacy, a few of the cousins and Celine, and Pam of course . . .'

The list went on, including the nice woman who cleans for him every Friday, his podiatrist and the postman. I started thinking it was basically everyone he'd spoken to in the past few days, and several people he would've had to go out of his way to encounter. I tuned back in when I sensed he was wrapping up, and he ended by confirming that the son of the man up the road who sells solid fuel was now also up to speed. I was, of course, delighted. As the ninth of eleven, there were very few landmarks of my life that were particularly momentous or memorable for Daddy. By the time of my arrival, my infant antics were probably a bit like watching those later Apollo missions, when they'd run out of ideas and just ended up driving around or doing step aerobics. My father ardently disputes that this is the case, but I have always presumed that after, say, number five or six, we all just collapsed into a mottled, whinging blur of nosebleeds and missing socks, an amorphous child-mass of sincerely loved but not necessarily individuated entities. I remember reading the scores of Christmas cards we received one year, when I was seven or eight, all addressed to *Joe O'Reilly & Family*, and working out that, in terms of total weight percentage, I barely constituted the dot over the i in the word 'Family'. If Hollywood, in their eternal search for propulsive thrills, were to make a film about us, I probably wouldn't even be a named character, instead listed in the credits as 'Second Fat Baby', or 'Crying Birthday Redhead'.

There were, of course, other benefits to Daddy spreading the word, and sitting with Patricia in Fermanagh, I now held some of them in my hand.

'Hold on to whatever,' she said as we sat down with a neat parcel of eleven letters, written in the last few years of Mammy's life. 'Sure, I know where they are. There's no rush.'

The first letter is dated 30 November 1987, just three weeks after the Remembrance Day bombings in which twelve people were killed by an IRA attack in Enniskillen.

'There's been so much sadness,' she wrote. 'Enniskillen really upset us all – I'll never forget that Sunday – it was like a nightmare – listening and watching. I was thinking of the past pupils' retreat and parking in there. I suppose the only hope is that good will come out of it.'

The letters Patricia gave me comprise less than five thousand words, and contain no direct mention of me at all. They cover my mother's near-constant visits to people in hospitals, or attendance at funerals, and the care she gave to Daddy's mother in the final stages of her life, eschewing the hospice in favour of letting her see out her days in the company of her grandchildren. They document her own illness too, and the changing fortunes of her battle with the cancer. But mostly they give encouragement, support and offers of prayerful solidarity to Patricia, alongside exhaustive updates on what we were all up to.

'Sinead is very busy with school,' she wrote in February 1991, 'she has also been in the school show *Brigadoon* and this week she's in the Operatic Society's *Carousel*. Dara is very involved with computers and the school magazine. Shane has joined a "very important" football team and spends a lot of time training. Maeve and Orla patiently await their 11+ results and we've been doing the rounds of "Open Days" at the local schools. All the others are busy in Nazareth House in their own way coping with the new curriculum. They're all very happy which means a lot. Sinead and Shane go to Germany during the Easter holidays. I'm supposed to be going too but apart from this setback, we have discovered that Maeve and Orla's confirmation is the day we come back so it's all very much up in the air at the moment.'

The setback she mentions is a lump in her neck, the third or fourth such growth in as many years. She did make it on the school jaunt in the end, but would never recover from this round of her illness, dying eight months later.

It seems profane to see her making plans and hoping for the best, but it's deeply touching that she wasn't mired in self-doubt and misery. More than anything else, the opportunity to see, to hold in my *hand*, something so clearly in my mother's voice was revelatory, and made me want to do more digging. Mammy had become, like Jesus or Derry City's league-winning side of 1989, one of those figures I didn't know personally, but recognised from being up on the walls of our house.

Patricia had been Mammy's first port of call with pregnancy announcements, although not by letter but via a morning phone call that might sometimes have been made before even Daddy was aware. Mammy always intuited she was pregnant very early, upon finding that the smell of her wake-up coffee made her nauseous. Many was the morning Patricia would receive the call before an abandoned brew had finished spiralling down my mother's sink. Patricia was on hand, not just because she was Mammy's best friend but because she always seemed delighted by the news, whereas other friends might have raised eyebrows at the increasing population of the O'Reilly household. It occurred to me quite late that this would have been a consideration: that it was something that my parents themselves would also have been, well, slightly embarrassed by.

It's odd that realising this about my parents took me so long, since I had worked out that we weren't like other families pretty early on. I'd noticed, for example, that my friends could recite their siblings' names without squinting or counting on their fingers. As a child, it was hard to avoid the implication that my parents were either out for an award from the pope or, at best, severely unimaginative when it came to other hobbies. It's not an area on which I'd like to dwell for too long, but neither is it one I can completely ignore, other than to say my parents were very Catholic, extremely fond of each other and had a deep commitment to, and love of, raising children. That being said, I don't think we were ever brought up to believe that we had all been deliberately conceived, and I find the idea that it would bother anyone either way rather strange. I remember watching TV dramas where a horrified child would scream in anguish at the suggestion they were an accident. To me, this seemed such an odd thing to care about, especially for a child – perhaps because it warranted them fondly imagining their parents planning sex. It was hard to imagine my parents sat there one night, looking at their eight children and thinking to themselves, 'we really ought to have one more at least'. I haven't – mercifully – thought about the actual circumstances that led to my conception, but I've got to presume forward planning wasn't much of a factor. What's important was that, once I arrived, I was loved and indulged and given all the small plastic dinosaurs any child could fit in a decorated cereal box.

I never really thought of it from Mammy and Daddy's point of view at the time, navigating the world as the parents of eleven children when it would have marked them out as at best mildly ridiculous and at worst deeply weird. This is why Mammy phoned Patricia before even her own mother. She'd noted congratulations from other quarters were growing a little more delayed. My mother loved having children – thank God – but she also lived in the modern world and understood that, as the numbers accumulated, each happy announcement might provoke greater surprise. By the last five or six blessings, this had transmuted to naked incredulity. For Granny McGullion, it came with hostility thrown in. It's amusing to think of my parents, neat and prim and well into their thirties, being chided like randy teenagers, but according to Patricia that's exactly what happened. Upon hearing that a fifth stork was flapping its wings toward our house, Granny McGullion is said to have uttered the words 'Joe O'Reilly, that brute!' Later, when they had a mere six children, Granny babysat while my parents spent a night in a hotel. As if waving her child off to a school dance, she gave Mammy a scolding reminder that they not take the opportunity to add to our number. The next morning, when my parents returned, Granny took Mammy aside and repeated her hope that this oath had been kept. I don't believe she'd even finished her censorious spiel before Mammy had tipped her coffee down the sink with abashed disgust.

Patricia later told me she did occasionally diverge from fulsome support, as when, two babies later, she took the caffeinated nausea call and betrayed her shock with an exclamation of 'Jesus Christ, Sheila', which stung my mother slightly.

'Oh, I thought you'd be pleased,' she said. 'You're always pleased when I'm pregnant.'

'Jesus, Mary and Joseph,' Patricia shot back, 'please don't think you have to keep doing it to make me happy.'

Undeterred, my mother went on to have three more children, the first of whom was me.

Mammy's people, like my father's, were all Fermanagh. Sheila McGullion was born into a cottage on the estate grounds of an Anglo-Irish farmer named George Tottenham, for whom my grandfather, James McGullion, worked as cattle master. Granda McGullion lived on site, in an arrangement that seems cut straight from the nineteenth century, but which continued until his retirement in the early seventies.

I never knew my grandmother, who died the year before I was born, but I was very fond of Granda, the only grandparent I can remember. He was a quiet man with a big face, and hair that seemed like a thick bush of white from afar but which, once you were sufficiently close, you could see was actually quite sparse. We often did get that close, since he often allowed us to comb it, slathering his big comb with Brylcreem and raking the gooey mess all over his hair, neck and scalp for what seemed like hours. There he would sit implacably, saying little and tolerating whichever cub or cuttie – the preferred Fermanagh terms for boys and girls – was pawing all over his hair like a stumpy little barber. No doubt he was delighted that he'd devised a play activity for which the only requirement from him was to sit down at the end of a tiring day. He had a tiny pair of wooden clogs which he would produce when we came over, and which he claimed belonged to a friend of his called Barney. Barney was a leprechaun and had a day job working in a sweet factory, giving his old pal Granda an exclusive inside line on those small rectangular boxes of Smarties which we were unaware you could buy in literally every shop on Earth.

Granda had the work ethic of a soldier ant, and well into his seventies would insist on earning his keep when he came to stay, trimming bushes, painting walls or doing other odd jobs. It was a joy to get to carry him out a pitcher of weak orange juice as he sheared at a hedge, working like a man who hadn't been born a few months before the *Titanic* sank.

The life of my mother's family seems odd to contemplate now, lived in a four-room cottage that was home not just to my mother and her parents, but also four siblings and, later, at least one ailing grandparent. As a child, I imagined them all sharing a big brass bed like the Bucket family in *Charlie and the Chocolate Factory*, their evenings spent peeling the one potato between them, washed down with pig's milk and a decade of the rosary. The strangeness of it is only increased when one considers further details, such as the preposterous deference that was to be shown by the family to the landowners for whom my grandfather worked. Mammy, for example, was encouraged to refer to Mr Tottenham's children, Ashley and Allison, who were broadly the same age as her, as Master Ashley and Miss Allison, even when they were all as young as five or six. It's hard for me to comprehend what my grandfather thought this would achieve, but whatever encouragement she was given to follow this practice, it didn't stick, and they had a close, non-hierarchical friendship in their later lives.

Tales of this cottage were one of the few things I'd been told about Mammy's near-parodically Irish childhood. Even describing it risks making me sound racist. In pictures, it looks like the kind of tiny house in which Irish people were depicted in Victorian cartoons, paid in pigs' feet and boiled cabbage, their only possessions bought with their winnings from leaping contests with the fairy folk. You can see it now in an engraving in your mind: the woman of the house a toothless slattern, scrubbing on a washboard while breastfeeding her seventeen children, all happy to work twenty hours a day licking the fields.

It wasn't quite on that level, I was told, but not far off. The house was small but was said to gleam, and Mrs McGullion was a proud and welcoming host. It had no fridge, so milk and vegetables were stored outside, and the floor had some form of lino covering, although its uneven surface suggested bare earth lay beneath. It goes without saying that an indoor toilet would have been regarded as a space-age luxury; such business was undertaken a sixty-second walk away, in the outhouse behind. Here, of course, came the glory of the place, as the latrine, and the house itself, backed on to the reckless beauty of Lough Erne's south-western reach, one of the more spectacular places on Earth you could hope to freeze your arse off.

This estate is now home to Blaney Spa and Yoga Centre, run by Gabriele, the widow of Ashley Tottenham — the aforementioned Master Ashley – who also died tragically young, a year or so before my mother. The old dwellings have been renovated into 'the Inishbeg Cottages', and are rented out to holidaymakers. A few months after receiving Patricia's letters, I set off to see the place. Here, I thought, was a chance to commune with the spirit of the dead, and rattle through questions for my dad, Patricia and any Fermanagh natives that would come out and meet us.

My wife and I drove down with my father so that I could fire questions at him on the way, in a more informal manner than the one I usually manage. My father loves to drive, so if you want to get decent dirt out of him it's a good way of going about it, disarming his usual reflex to bat away questions like a dodgy builder evading a reporter from *Watchdog*. The trip to my mother's birthplace took us through a lot of the places of my father's own childhood, which allowed him to indulge in some rare moments of nostalgia en route. Belleek is an idyllic, lough-strewn corner of Northern Ireland which, from most angles, looks almost ludicrously pretty. Fermanagh might be the least talked-about county in Ireland. You rarely meet people from there or hear about them on the news. I reckon there are people who've lived there all their lives and are still not sure that it's a real place.

I'd say it was a place of entirely unspoiled natural beauty except that, like the whole of Northern Ireland, its history and landscape are pockmarked by the grisly tumult of the seventies and eighties, not least the Enniskillen bombings, which took place just two years after my parents moved fifty miles north to Derry and had me, their favoured son, and my two younger siblings. Belleek is best known for the pottery that bears its name, and rather less so for being the most westerly settlement in the United Kingdom. It is what tourists think all Irish towns are like, a place so handsomely quaint it seems unreal. If it were a comic, its origin story would be that of a normal town bitten by a radioactive watercolour painting. You can, even now, stand on any random electrical box in Belleek and whatever photograph you'd take could be framed and sold to an elderly American ten minutes later.

My father's people were Fermanagh going back; the O'Reillys arrived in the county in the eighteenth century. O'Reillys are synonymous with neighbouring Cavan, where legend – and 90 per cent of keyrings found in local gift shops – tells us they were a storied and impressive people, the high kings of East Brefni. There is, to this day, some contention over even this appellation, since both the O'Rourkes and the O'Reillys have claimed to be *the* princes of Brefni in a beef that's been going for the past seven hundred years. It's pleasing to report that, as late as 1994, a ruling was made granting that title to the O'Rourkes over my own forebears. In one tantalising line, Wikipedia informs me that 'in 2017, with the election of the new O'Reilly Chief, the rivalry has been rekindled'. I was happy to inform my dad that he may well be drafted into a heraldic war at some point in the near future.

Whatever the facts of the matter, my father is much given to saying that the O'Reillys made the journey to Fermanagh 'by coach-and-four', which, to him, implies a certain regality that must, considering our own diminished means, have been substantially watered down in the succeeding centuries. It's his favourite part of the story, and so he was mildly annoyed when my brother Conall made him explain for all our benefit what exactly that meant.

'Four horses!' he proclaimed, indignant at our indifference to our high-status origins. 'Sure the queen herself has only six,' he added, the latest volley in his impressive, life-long pursuit of metrics by which we and the Windsors might be compared. My father's interest in genealogy flourished during his fifties when, in place of the time, means or opportunity to have a full-blown midlife crisis, he became suddenly desirous of knowing everything he could about our family tree. It's from this period he managed to date the time of this Cavan-to-Fermanagh migration as 1724 to 1774.

'Long trip,' said Conall.

The O'Reilly and McGullion dynasties were joined in 1972, when my parents married. At the ceremony, Patricia turned to Granny to say how beautiful the bride looked in her gown and fur stole. Resolutely unmoved, the elder Mrs O'Reilly is said to have replied, 'I just hope she doesn't spend all of Joe's money,' presumably before chasing a tomcat out of the church by banging on some pots and pans. She did become immensely fond of my mother, and if she shared Granny McGullion's angst about the number of children they were having, no such indication was ever given. Certainly, she appears to have been a much more doting grandmother than she was a schoolmistress for my father.

My mother's birthplace is a little different from when she knew it. I pop into the yoga centre to grab the keys and find that morning's class of chakra-centred septuagenarians sipping juice and coffee on the sun-drenched porch overlooking Lough Erne.

A woman named Hope approaches, squinting meaningfully at my face as though I'm an eye chart that's slightly too far away.

'Oh my gosh, you're like her,' she says, meaning my mother, who, it turns out, she used to catch the bus to school with as a child. 'I can see her reflection in you,' she reiterates, and as we talk I catch faint ripples of amazement in her eyes, struck by that uncanny sense of seeing the face of one long gone in someone else.

'So, you're digging up the roots?' she says as I describe my trip.

'Yes,' I reply. 'I guess I am.'

We are shown inside my mother's house, which is between renovations. I'm struck by how big it is really, since I had probably internalised a little too much of my own spiel and was expecting to find somewhere the size of a spice rack, not this two-storey cottage which, though likely a tight fit for eight, is considerably larger than my flat. My dad tells me how it looked when he last saw it in the early seventies, gesturing to long-gone fittings and appliances, rearranging the floorplan with points and waves. 'I was never allowed upstairs, of course,' he reminds us, since his last visits would have been before they were married, and he a good Catholic boy. It's my wife who has the presence of mind to discreetly challenge him on this point once we ascend the staircase and find that he is miraculously able to show us how the top floor looked as well. 'I suppose you'll be putting that in the book,' he says, not unjustly, for about the eightieth time that afternoon.

Mammy's house looks out on a view of the lough in all its magnificence; dotted islands, darting, diving swifts and the distant reeling of anglers, languidly drifting along the glassy lake. The hills round here don't so much roll as jump in great big blobs, looking for all the world like children's toys hastily swept under a dark green rug. Fermanagh is like Ireland in miniature; its vistas wide, its towns tidy, its 4G variable. Its lack of coastline is more than made up for by the long, winding, spectacular grandeur of the lough and the 365 islands that lie within. The Erne is split into two portions, Upper and Lower, but in a fit of confusing nomenclature that is very much a Fermanagh trademark these are situated paradoxically, with the Lower 'above' its Upper counterpart on the map. My father takes great delight in telling me this, since he spent forty years with the Northern Irish Water Service as an engineer. This trip handily combines three of his specialist subjects: the extraordinary natural beauty of his home county; the intricacies of Northern Ireland's waterways; and schooling his know-it-all son in things about which he actually knows nothing.

Patricia said she thought my mum gained her calm from this place. My mother's calm is something everyone mentions about her, the stoical resolve with which she tackled life, marriage, parenthood and her illness, and it pervades the letters she sent to Patricia, which I bring with me. 'I am not the bearer of great news,' she wrote in October 1988.

'It appears the cancer has recurred, and the doctors consider the best step is to have a full mastectomy. I'm going to the Royal tomorrow Thurs 20th, for surgery Friday ... Emotionally at best I'm disappointed – it was really the last thing I expected at this stage, God's ways certainly aren't my ways. I don't understand what's happening, I'm upset but I'm still hopeful. I'm banking a lot on Mr Charles – of all the legions of people recommended to me he's the one I really feel drawn to. I know I don't have to ask for your prayers not only for me but especially Joe – he is really devastated. We told the children last night and they were great – so practical, who'd do what for them, when and where? We told Sinead and Dara the whole situation and they were very accepting – they've been expecting me to go to Belvoir [a specialist cancer facility in Belfast] anyhow. Shane and Mairead would show more emotion but once they got over that they were okay. Shane is going with St Eugene's Cathedral Choir to the National Concert Hall on Saturday 29th, but maybe the concerts competition is on Sunday I'm not sure. God bless, Sheila.'

Her religious faith is evident throughout the letters, and stretched not merely to church attendance and ancillary responsibilities but to listening to tapes of Catholic mystics like Sister Briege McKenna as she did little jobs about the place. 'I was down seeing Daddy yesterday,' she wrote in March 1990, 'and on the way there and back I listened to tapes of Briege McKenna. Over and over again she repeats "come to me you who are burdened and finding life difficult and I will give you rest and refresh you". She even goes so far as to say that many people go with their troubles to psychiatrists when they can so easily tell all their worries and heartaches to God!' Reading these letters, it's disarming to imagine my mother driving around these very hills, nodding along to the homespun wisdom of some nuns on tape. I suppose these were a charming early precursor to podcasts, aimed at philosophical Catholics with a lot of errands to run. My mother fitted that remit on both counts. These errands too are a constant reference point, as in the earlier missive that sees Mammy segue from surgery to my brother Shane's choir trip to Dublin the following week.

Her faith also informed the advice she gave, including one odd moment of spontaneous scripture recommendation:

'[B]e assured of a continuing presence in our thoughts and prayers. Don't give up. As I was writing I was trying to pray and Matthew 14 kept coming into my head. I don't know what's in it and I'm not accustomed to scripture gifts like this but I'll take a chance and tell you anyhow. I hope it brings you consolation.'

I never did think to ask Patricia if Matthew 14, the chapter Mammy appears to have conjured out of thin air as an impromptu 'scripture gift', offered any consolation. In the end, I thought better of it, since upon looking it up I found it tells the story of Christ feeding the five thousand, so it may merely give her unwelcome reminders of all those times Mammy, Daddy and we, their eleven tired and hungry children, had arrived to eat her out of house and home.

Granny McGullion died of cancer in 1984, a few years before the first of these letters, and her suffering had had a huge effect on my grandfather and Mammy. Neither of them ever actually admitted it was cancer at all, and Mammy and her siblings were even instructed by Granny and Granda to tell people it was glandular fever. I guess they didn't want to give the thing power by naming it, as if saying the word cancer out loud would make it real, somehow. It's also true that they didn't want to suffer the pity of outsiders or cause any fuss in their ordinary interactions with people. This last concept is the one I find easiest to believe, since fuss, in all its forms, is like kryptonite to Northern Irish people.

It's an odd thing to realise how much of your homeland you've internalised, the unspoken assumptions, latent behaviours and rigid rhythms of thought that were baked into your breast before you were conscious it was happening. So it is with fuss. Fuss means different things to different people, and it has to since, where I come from, fuss is a particularly pejorative term. Watching American TV shows in which loud, self-possessed people complained about their meals, for example, was as exotic as watching people using jetpacks on *Tomorrow's World*. We are, after all, a population who lived through a period in which some 10 per cent of us lost an immediate family member to political violence and saw fit to call this era the Troubles, as if it were not a brutal cycle of spiteful bloodshed but rather a period of intemperate hailstorms, or a breakdown in the country's system of planning applications.

'Don't make a fuss', 'it's no big deal', 'ah sure, lookit the horse has bolted, what good will whining do?' These were platitudes we lived by on the micro and the macro scale, the sorts of things people would say upon being offered a cup of tea, or receiving an unsatisfactory dinner in a restaurant, but would also feel in our hearts when faced with death or trauma or the abject desolation of being alone in an unfeeling world. It could never be *said* that it is indulgent or improper to speak at length about grief or death; it was just roundly felt and universally known to be the case, as surely as you wouldn't extemporise on the ugliness of someone's spouse. Within this heuristic there was, of course, an internal spectrum, just as there are, presumably, New Yorkers who will sit happily silent with a hair in their lasagne.

The arc of sensibility in Northern Ireland bends away from fuss, and it has bent that way inside me since my childhood. It's one of the reasons I'm more comfortable talking about death in terms of its comical absurdities, in the odd contradictions and baffling misapprehensions that come in its wake. I talk about my family's experience a lot, and shrink rapidly from any hint that I'm being too grave or serious while doing so. Far be it from me to make my family's tragedy seem like something that was actually sad. The more I think and talk about the events of my life, the more I think on this horror of fuss and consider it the part of myself, and my homeland, that I would like to change above all others.

When Granda McGullion retired, in a move that, depending on who you talk to, was either par for the course or callous towards an old man, he had to leave Blaney, since the house came with the job. Certainly, Granda never held it against his employers and respected and admired the Tottenhams until his dying day. The feeling was very much mutual, particularly for Ashley, who adored the McGullions. 'They always had a little light in the window,' Gabriele tells me he was fond of saying. 'He loved going there.'

The day before, I had been about to tell her about the letter my mother had written to Patricia in tribute to Ashley, when she produced a photocopy of it herself, a gift from Patricia some years earlier. It reflects how much my mother thought about people other than herself, even when going through unimaginable stress.

'I hope to go to Fermanagh tomorrow to see Daddy for Easter,' she wrote. 'He's in good form but was very saddened to hear of Ashley Tottenham's death, do you remember him? His first wife died and he then married a German girl who had been an assistant at the Convent & College. He was diagnosed with stomach cancer, just after me and put up a great fight. He was only 37. I had been talking to him a lot any time I was down home because he was always interested to see how I was doing. Thank God I'm fine.'

8

The Forge

The large, white, five-bedroom bungalow in which I was raised was sometimes called the Forge by my father, and literally no one else. This soubriquet is lovingly rendered on letters my dad sends to relatives, conferring a certain elegance of standing. The Forge could be a fancy B&B, the summer residence of a timber baron, or a stately home that's been converted into a rehab centre for celebrity drug addicts.

It actually takes its name from its being set on a plot of land once used by a blacksmith, a fact pleasingly confirmed if you dig a hole anywhere around our garage, where you will find all manner of shrapnel, pig iron and horse shoes. The field behind the house once verged on the UK customs checkpoint, but after the demilitarisation of the border that was shut down and the land, together with the top bit of our field, was sold to build a family home for some new neighbours. My father planted trees to provide a barrier, as he did along two hundred metres stretching from the garage to the slope at the front of the house that has farmland on both sides. This second line of trees was essentially planted to keep the horse in Toland's field from eating my dad's flowers but, in the age of Brexit, it has now risen to the exalted position of being fully 0.04 per cent of the United Kingdom's border with the European Union. Such a promotion might seem slightly above the paygrade of some mottled conifers and a fence you could knock over with a few harsh words. And if you ask that horse if it's a solid barrier, he'll tell you no. He may even do so from my dad's flower beds, in between bites of nasturtium.

So, my family home is not merely on the border, it is a structural part of it, but none of that was of interest during my childhood because it was just my house and, for the most part, the border thing was largely irrelevant.

The land around the house is uncommonly pleasant: rolling hills, fields and open farmland pretty much as far as the eye can see. The hills in the distance are actually across the River Foyle, which itself isn't visible from my home, although if you were to walk the short road down to Balloughry it's so quiet you can hear the noise of the traffic as it passes along the far side. There's wildlife here: wood pigeons, pheasant, large game birds and mid-sized raptors, along with the usual but slightly less commonly sighted owls, foxes and badgers. There are cows in the fields perhaps half the year, and a thin, scraggly electric wire separates their parish from ours where the slope meets the fence and our land terminates. The wire gives a faint electric shock that is barely painful, but enough to alarm cattle into thinking twice about ascending onto our property, and for the most part they seem to take no interest in us at all. Sometimes, however, the cows spontaneously develop some irresistible, albeit temporary, obsession with us, and congregate right at that fence. One or two mornings a year we'd throw back the living-room curtains to find forty-five cows staring with listless attention, like world-weary reporters summoned to a press conference about council tax increases.

Once or twice they've ventured further and have, in confused ebullience, stormed the fence and run around our house in a spiral of panic, perhaps in some thirst for the freedom of gravel and pebbledash denied to them in the field. To look out of our kitchen window and see a churning mass of dead-eyed cattle circling the house is thrilling. I've never forgotten my sister Caoimhe loudly screaming at me to close the door. This I did, but not before imagining – with delight – dirty-hooved cows storming into our house and running around for no reason. Thankfully/alas, this never happened, and any time they did break through the perimeter we would just ring the farmer and he'd come and apologise and I'd get to watch as he shooed them back down to their field with some uncanny authority that our own screams somehow lacked.

Where I grew up is, in short, the kind of place you might see on *Grand Designs* before a really annoying couple erect a black cement monstrosity their neighbours will hate, complete with arty windows made specially in Germany that arrive two months late and way over budget. The view from the back of our house is dotted with distant houses and tall windmills that look down over the north-eastern banks of the Foyle. It's gloriously picturesque, giving the scene from our living-room window the near-perfect charm of a Windows Desktop wallpaper. As a child, of course, all of this was lost on me, since I had about as much interest in scenery as I had in *BBC Parliament*. When I'm back home these days I can barely keep my eyes off the landscape, stunned into slack-jawed amazement, not just at the view itself, but at the fact I lived within it for most of my childhood and didn't give it a second thought.

Most but not all of my childhood, that is. I was once an avid agriculturalist. Aged six, a short while after my mother's death, I became obsessed with the idea of becoming a farmer. I was in it for the machines and was besotted with tractors most of all. I had several myself, all different sizes, as if caught at different stages of their life cycle. I had very small ones that I could plot on little model farmyards of various scales, then I had slightly larger ones with moving trailers and attachments, which I could push by hand. I then had big ones, in which I could sit and pedal myself around, usually still holding a good selection of those other tractors in my lap, just in case at any point while riding round on my tractor I needed a quick reminder of just how much I loved tractors. I wore wellies, quilted gilets and flat caps while driving around pointing at things I wanted to farm. What exactly constituted farming was, to me, somewhat hazy, but I guessed it was basically riding on my tractor while saying 'ey up' to dogs and nudging everything I saw with the digger attachment. Long days of this grew tiring for both me and the people and things I was trying to farm out of the way, but the life of a farmer is not for the faint hearted. And so, the dog was farmed, my siblings were farmed, and any random objects that I encountered also farmed. I received tractor calendars for Christmas and would turn the pages excitedly on the first morning of every month, delighted to find whatever new model was there waiting for me. It bothered me that these calendars were invariably sold by the manufacturers themselves, and so would only show makes from said manufacturer. Brand loyalty meant less to me than variety. Craving a mix of tractors each month, I soon had a John Deere calendar and a Massey Ferguson one, hung side by side, so as to give me the broad diet I deserved.

I was in awe of my dad's friend Robert, who farmed down the road and used to come by our house in his tractor and let me look at it. I was incredibly impressed with my dad for knowing a real live farmer who would come to our house and say hello. To six-year-old me, this was like a greeting from God. I idolised him to such an extent that I'd get too sheepish to talk, and would instead show my appreciation by taking his wellies once he'd removed them and storing them by the door in the back hall, in an act of wordless, admiring servitude. I would probably have been delighted to wash them for him. One day my dad arranged for Robert to take me farming for the day. To date, this is probably still the greatest thrill I've ever experienced. He picked me up at 6 a.m., and I was given a glimpse of the heady glamour of driving through fields, feeding hay to cows and getting waves from other farmers as we went past. I tipped my cap and waved back, making it clear that I too was one of their tribe, since they probably couldn't make out all the tractors in my lap that would have proved it beyond all doubt.

By the time I started school this passion had faded. I grew out of wellies that were never replaced, and the once-endless supply of nested tractor toys gathered dust before being tidied away for ever. When Robert visited, his wellies remained untouched, and I barely looked up when we heard the gravel crunch of his big fat tyres coming in. By the time I was seven or eight, I was not merely indifferent but actively hostile to the environment. The glory and splendour of the countryside existed, as far as I could tell, solely to provide me with knobbly sticks I could hit things with as I walked along low walls. We defaced trees with our initials and, later, blighted them with our own half-baked Grand Designs: our numerous futile attempts to make tree-forts.

My father was a maker of things, a trained architect and an engineer. His father had been a carpenter. I, on the other hand, was never bitten by the woodworking bug, and certainly not one that would have instantaneously granted me the powers of a master craftsman which, in truth, was what I wanted. What I've always wanted: to be good at something while committing as little time, effort and attention to it as possible. I wanted to learn things as quickly as it took a spirited montage to finish: was this so much to ask? A childhood spent watching films in which scrappy gangs of misfits manufacture outwardly ramshackle but entirely viable mansions in trees had led me and my siblings to believe we'd just kind of get the hang of building a treehouse as we went. All we had to do, it seemed, was carry wood to the area and occasionally hammer things until, hey presto, by the end of a Huey Lewis song you'd have a fully finished four-bed clubhouse ready to hold meetings in.

It turned out that there were several steps in between 'wanting to build a treehouse' and 'having the finished article installed safely in situ'. Safety wasn't even the big concern; we were more than happy for the thing to be a death trap so long as it was recognisably a structure and not a sad assemblage of rotting branches, buttressed by planks we'd stolen from our own beds. The end result would be a precarious platform of damp, angular plywood that provided no shelter – we never got to the point where a roof was a likely prospect – and was significantly more uncomfortable to sit in than the tree limbs we'd just built over. Our best attempts looked like fences that had been blown away in a gale and become lodged in a tree, rather than something that was deliberately placed there by human design. Nevertheless, we'd still spend a few hours sitting in this mangled arrangement, as if hoping to convince ourselves that it had been time well spent. 'Ah,' we'd say, our knees bent round the accessible part of an out-jutting plank, feeling it crack and groan under our weight. 'This is the life.' After each attempt, we'd go back inside disillusioned, vowing never to try again, and it would be a few weeks before Daddy worked out why our mattresses kept collapsing out of our bedframes.

We had miles of greenery around us to amble through but settled instead on caking ourselves in dirt and leaves by tumbling down the slope behind the house – the one that bordered on the cows – as an improvised slide. The electric fence that sat at the bottom of this slope should have been a disincentive, but we were no fools – we knew that we were protected from hitting the fence by the thick barrier of stinging nettles that we rolled into instead. We climbed trees and poked at streams. We traipsed through hedges looking for blackberries. We really wanted to find caterpillars that we'd keep as pets. We'd store them in a jar, which we would invariably forget about, only to discover some months later a grisly glass prison of exploded, furry mould. Nowadays, I'm incapable of holding myself back from rambling through the square mile that traces around our house, down towards the river, swinging right to trace the path over the border and towards the nearby village of Carrigans.

The entire time I do this, I'm constantly chattering to my wife or anyone else foolish enough to accompany me, loudly lamenting my own inability as a child to see this very real wood for these very real trees, when I would have covered the entire countryside in concrete if it meant a chance of a cinema or a Laser Quest setting up nearby. It's a conversation I'm sure they relish.

Despite my rural upbringing, I feel as though I developed very little kinship with nature. The only time I did feel like a proper country boy was when friends from the city would come out and not know how to climb over cattle fences or tramp through paths without getting their runners muddy. I'd laugh at their fear of large, stupid cows and lie about the names of trees and birds we'd encounter. I never got caught until one day I couldn't identify an oak, which is probably the only tree that every person in Derry knows since it's the official tree of the county. To me, knowing all the names for trees would have been as pointless as a city boy remembering every brand of satellite dish on his road. Of course, I had even less need to memorise a hundred types of dinosaur, or star, or prime number, but I did all that – because I was an indoor kid at heart.

The front door of our house was reserved exclusively for trades-people, postmen and visiting priests. The back hall was the real anteroom, as well as the area in which phone calls were chiefly made, with the little table common to every home in the Irish countryside, on which stood the phone, the phone book, a torch and a rack of keys (perhaps 4 per cent of which were identifiable). We had a religious icon over the door, a tiny little Blessed Virgin with a font of holy water at her feet, guaranteeing protection for all who passed over our threshold.

For most of my younger days, it was nearly impossible to use the phone when I wanted, since my sisters spent most evenings calling a revolving cast of friends with great urgency, mere hours after they had last been sighted, safe and well, at school. The phone table itself was the most uncomfortable place to sit in our entire house. Possibly to dissuade us from near-constant use of the phone, it was as ill-shaped and wonky as one of our treehouses, almost as if Daddy had intended it as a piece of hostile architecture, the way city planners put those spiked benches in bus stations so homeless people can't sleep on them. Despite this measure, my father was accustomed to picking up the phone by his armchair to hear one of his daughters angsting to a pal, as if the line was permanently connected to a switchboard for disaffected Northern Irish youths. When the internet was installed, it worked off the same phone line, meaning it was now not just permanently engaged, but also emitted an ear-splitting electronic screech if you haplessly picked up the receiver. In those days the internet was charged like a phone call, meaning that one month early in my use of the service I racked up over £100 of charges. I wish I could even claim it was for some agreeably salacious use, but I was mostly concerned with reading rumours about the new *Star Wars* prequels and downloading *South Park* sound clips.

Once a hub within our home, in the aftermath of the landline's demise the back hall has become little more than a vestibule for various items of outerwear to be quickly grabbed if you need to go outside into the garage. There are roughly a thousand discarded shoes, and a mat for the dog, who is allowed to sleep there when she gets scared by the many things that now appear to terrify her very greatly indeed. There is a coat rack by the far wall which holds – and I have counted – twenty-eight coats, jackets, fleeces and items of hi-viz apparel, all of which at one point or another may have been in daily use by one or several of us, but which were for years kept as a last resort should someone need something to wear when nipping out for a fag. None of us live there any more, nor do we smoke when we return, so this stock of coats has been frozen in time since, I would reckon, about 2009. A recent dig through the archaeological strata uncovered a coat I'd forgotten ever owning, a tatty army surplus thing, its pockets containing a few crumbles of weed and a USB stick of bad techno.

The back hall opens onto the kitchen, where the first thing that greets you is the twelve-foot-long table that has served as the locus of family life for thirty-five years. It's the first sign that you're entering a house that was designed to accommodate my family's ludicrous dimensions. It has a marble-effect top, which was probably meant to seem classy but looks more like the backdrop for the cover of a mid-nineties rap album. It was the venue for all the family meals we had together growing up, was the centre point of Christmas dinners, and is now the favoured spot for late-night drinking sessions when we end up at home together. The dogs like to sit underneath it. The steady hum and hiss of their snoring, accompanied by Italian football on Channel 4 and the dishwasher working its way through the dinnerplates we'd just used, was the soundtrack to my every childhood Sunday. That is until I started blaring the Aphex

Twin and Autechre CD-Rs that would send Daddy in to rip the speaker plug from the wall.

After Mammy died, a kitchen rota was enforced that split chores up among us, ostensibly to cover the shortfall engendered by her death. This was slightly odd since our housekeeper, Anne, did most of the daily cleaning, but it did help at weekends and after dinner, while also instilling a bit of discipline for its own sake. The rota, famously devised by Maeve and Orla, ruled out the Big Ones since they were busy studying for exams, and instituted a master/apprentice system by which a Middle One and a Wee One were paired to split the cleaning tasks for the day; one washing, one drying, one sweeping, one picking up, etc. This kitchen rota was widely praised by adult observers, but also passed into O'Reilly lore as a wretched tale of forced labour and exploitation. It was common for the older siblings to treat the younger as willing servants, and to capitalise on their inexperience for their own gain. When time came to clean the bedroom they shared, Mairead convinced Dearbhaile, two years her junior, to split the room down the middle. This would have been a fair arrangement had Mairead not decreed that the dividing line would separate the room's top and bottom halves, meaning Dearbhaile cleaned the entire room, leaving Mairead to make the bed on her own top bunk. Not that I was above such sharp practice myself. On the rare occasions we were gifted money, I kept a pot of 2p coins set aside that I could trade for any £1 coins Conall received, on the basis that the 2p coins were much larger and this must constitute greater value.

The rota was different in that it was systematic and operated in plain sight. The Middle Ones (then aged nine to thirteen) were a bit more savvy than their infant charges (aged two to seven) and wielded their power in a microcosm of capitalist malfeasance. Soon they had tricked us into doing almost all the work while they watched. So it was that a Middle One might put away the dishes after their partner had collected, washed and dried them.

Over on the far wall, beside the dishwasher, there used to be a serving hatch that opened into the dining room, which was by far the coolest thing in our house. Daddy got rid of it in a subsequent renovation, but I don't think I've ever forgiven him, even though there was literally no reason that we would need a portal from the kitchen into the dining room since we ate all our meals in the kitchen, and very few objects were transferred from one room to the other, least of all those that were small enough to get through a hole that size. It was just cool. The disappearance of this little hole, smaller and way less useful than a door, united us in grief. Usually, you'd just open it to see what was going on in the dining room, only to find that it was, as usual, empty, or else occupied by a single, annoyed person, wondering why you'd opened the hatch to stare at them. It remains much missed.

The dining room itself is one of those things, like damp or bats, that are ubiquitous in rural Irish homes; rooms which are lavishly appointed but never used for their designated purpose. Not only did we never dine in there, it would stretch credulity for me to even imagine doing so. Having dinner in the dining room would be like watching TV in the hall or sleeping on the bathroom floor; a category error so flamboyantly unhinged it doesn't bear thinking about. It housed a table and a grand dresser filled with plates and cups and all manner of other bric-a-brac deemed fancy or irrelevant. The good crockery therein was only used for very special visitors, either to make it clear that they were very special visitors or else give the impression that we were so profoundly fancy that we spent every evening drinking from perfectly unspoiled cups with a tiny gold rim, rather than those we actually used, which were a chipped mass of ceramic scrap bearing the logos of different chocolate bars we got in a few decades' worth of Easter eggs. The room was used for every other conceivable purpose than eating or looking at the nice plates. It's where we used the internet over the aforementioned achingly slow dial-up connection. It's where my little brother and I played computer games or watched un-family-friendly TV programmes. We used it for music practice as it contained a piano and about twenty dozen other instruments accumulated during my dad's unflagging efforts to make musicians of us all. These stuck around for decades after we either left or stopped playing, meaning that if you stood up too quickly the entire room made a faint twanging, plinking, hooting noise, as if you'd startled a very small chamber orchestra. The dresser that contained the fancy plates was also slowly filled with bottles of whiskey my father was gifted by unimaginative friends and colleagues who didn't realise he drank only one or two tumblers of whiskey per year, nor that his children would happily drain them for him. Nowadays, it serves as a makeshift spare bedroom for Christmases and other gatherings that exceed the allotted occupancy of the house. We've all at one time or another found ourselves on the singularly uncomfortable fold-out bed, drifting off to sleep with a prestigious view of what instruments now remain, as well as some of the finest plates in the parish.

*

The living room – also known as the sitting room or, more commonly in Derry parlance, the good room – is my favourite room in the house, featuring its greatest asset: the grand, south-facing eight-metre-square window that looks out over a beautiful scene of County Derry and Donegal. We like to say that it faces the Foyle, but it actually more directly faces Reservoir Meats, the meat-processing plant on its northmost bank, where both of my older brothers held summer jobs in their teens, and which luckily is also too distant to be visible. On the hills to the south-east are several gigantic wind turbines that add a futuristic majesty to the view which otherwise would look like something from a cover of *Ireland's Own*. The good room was where we gathered to watch TV and work our way through Daddy's vast, vast collection of video tapes.

Certain governing laws were true of those long sunny days when *Raiders of the Lost Ark* had just come on, or the second half of the FA Cup was set to kick off. It was an absolute certainty that such a moment would be the cue for the compressed, crackly hiss of an unfamiliar car driving into the front yard, which meant visitors.

When we were small, and so starved of attention and distraction we voluntarily spent time with our siblings, the prospect of visitors, no matter how mundane, was something to be celebrated. Even if it was one of Daddy's friends from prayer group, or a local eccentric who assembled wicker popes in his spare time, we would receive them as emissaries from the wider universe as gratefully as if we'd been manacled to the furniture and barred from all outside contact. But this glad, happy feeling toward visitors had switched off entirely by the time we reached twelve, at which point we greeted the prospect of guests with unsurpassed dread. By that age, all adults seem so preposterously boring that if Neil Armstrong himself had arrived, fresh from the moon and carrying several species of lunar spider he wanted to show us, we would have cursed the interruption, since it would more than likely have arrived at just the time when we were enjoying doing something else or – bliss itself – nothing at all.

Once we heard that crunch of gravel, we were quickly drummed to action stations. In an ecstasy of nervy fumbling, four of us would scatter to the kitchen with the kind of haste that wraps your heart around your back. Daddy would answer the door and we prepared the hospitality required. The most senior present would cut up some of the ubiquitous fruitcake. Another would be on biscuit assembly, laying an appetising selection of our fanciest biscuits on a plate. Convention dictated that one circular biscuit (a Coconut Ring, Jammie Dodger or Toffee Pop, in ascending order of fanciness) went in the centre, with auxiliary circle and oblong biscuits radiating outward from the middle in a floral burst, a brown and beige mandala that screamed refinement.

Whoever wasn't immediately necessary for arranging or preparing food would also decamp to the kitchen, not out of any great desire to be helpful but in the hope that this feeble pantomime of bustling activity would legitimise their having left the sitting room, for entertaining visitors could be an awkward affair. Most visits were punctuated by long silences scored by deafening clock ticks and tea slurps off the good china. A deadening series of bulletins was delivered as to the visitor's well-being, and that of their children and other family members, as if my father was the overseer of a minor fiefdom, one who demanded from his subjects not gold nor grain but news of each child's academic progress and extravagantly detailed descriptions of the elders' medical ailments. Barney, it turns out, had done the 11+ now and had actually done quite well in the language section, which was fascinating because he'd gone into the exam thinking it would be the maths that saw him through.

At the time, of course, I had neither the imagination nor the empathy to realise that my father had no more wish to converse with these people than we did. It never occurred to me that Daddy would, or could, be bored in the company of other adults. I simply didn't think he had the good sense to be. When considered sanely, adult life – with its radio documentaries, coffee breaks and HP sauce – was so incongruously, immorally bleak, so staggeringly lacking in diversion, that it strongly suggested adults were incapable of identifying pleasant experiences and were simply dead to all joy. A bit like how dogs don't mind living outside, or French people like France. Surely, if they were in possession of the slightest discernment, there'd be much less time dedicated to attending Mass, voluntarily listening to country music or making trips to the dump. How could one justify their frankly insane lack of interest in sitting upside down on sofas?

It seemed as though all adults everywhere were engaged in a heartless competition to be more insufferably boring than each other, just so they could be left in peace. These interactions were the perfect example of this evil art. They featured my father's full vocabulary of impressive, noncommittal tics: rapid intakes of breath, flattening jumper folds, scratching placemats with index fingers, more rapid intakes of breath but this time while saying 'this is it' or 'there we are' or 'ah sure anyway', each of these offered with the absent-minded air you have when the cashier is asking you if you do Nectar points, and you're boiling to get home for a shite. It is, of course, illegal for an Irish person to say, or even imply, that they'd like a guest to leave their home. If a friend were to arrive on your doorstep, covered in pigshit and carrying an open container of the SARS virus, you would still have to offer him a cup of tea at least twice. Once in your home, a guest must be made to feel welcome for as long as is humanly bearable.

Perhaps this is why my father would so routinely get us to perform for guests, since the idea that several children belting out an off-key Irish ballad was genuine entertainment seems outlandish. These recitals were often not enough, and the performances would be followed by more offers of tea and biscuits and fruitcake. At some point the exchange of mangled fricatives would slow down, and the pace of throat clearings and mumbled half-answers would increase, indicating the universally recognised consensus that a social interaction is drawing to a close. The endpoint would be the slap of the thigh and a fondly intoned 'Right!' before standing up and exhaling, in a gesture which is about as close to shooting your guest out of a cannon as is legally permitted.

Our bedrooms were nicely turned out, and after a few chops and changes as the family grew, their order of occupants froze after my mother's death, so that we all stayed in the same place until we packed off for university and left home for good. Most of them have since been done up, so they no longer bear the bunk beds and decals that I can list from memory: the posters in my sisters' room declaring Fionnuala's ardent love for the unlikely pairing of Liverpool player Jason McAteer and Saracen from *Gladiators*; the glow-in-the-dark Casper the Friendly Ghost stickers that were released as part of a cereal box promotion for the 1995 film and somehow ended up a permanent feature of Dearbhaile's bed, despite the fact that, to the best of my knowledge, she had no particularly deep commitment to said film.

Because we all did quite well in school, people tend to assume my dad was a taskmaster. Friends confess they thought he must have been the pushy type; a field marshal who kept us in a perpetual state of readiness ahead of the next impromptu pop quiz. 'Oh, I'll pass you the butter,' he might say at the breakfast table, 'but only if you first tell me how accurate it would be to describe the decline of the crusader states as being primarily due to the quality of Saladin's leadership in the years 1169–87.' Nothing could be further from the truth. He hoped we would do well, of course, but I don't think he ever knew what subjects I was doing, nor who any of my teachers were. One of the few benefits of being the widowed father of eleven children was that when he refused to perform the mundane and pointless obligations expected of other parents, nobody dared object. It was customary for teachers to send every student home with a daybook describing their behaviour, to be signed by a parent every night. In it would be written comments like 'Séamas kept whistling the theme music to *Pet Rescue*' or 'Séamas was sarcastic to the school dog' and your parent was supposed to read these and admonish you, and then sign the thing so your teacher knew that it was sorted. Loads of boys in my class just signed their own, but I think I was the only person who was actively encouraged to do so by my father, who simply lacked the necessary bandwidth to care about such details, let alone to do so for eight or nine children every single night. I did forge his signature for a while, but pretty soon I just stopped signing it altogether. My teacher never minded because, well, who wants to be the one bothering Joe O'Reilly? This suited my dad, who had several thousand other things to worry about, fine, and it most certainly suited me.

What Daddy might have lacked in a minute-by-minute, hands-on approach to my schooling, he made up for with more practical acts of ingenuity. He deliberately raised us in an incredibly uneventful part of the countryside, with nothing to do for miles around.

I was too young to remember the time the IRA blew up the customs hut at the top of our field, and would entertain fantasies, both fond and frequent, of more explosions coming our way to break the tedium. It didn't seem fair that the city types had all the fun. Even a kidnapping or a chase would have been welcome, for God's sake. It would be some years before we even accrued the few neighbours we have there now, so at weekends, if we weren't grumbling as we helped Daddy cut grass or fix gutters, we would loll about in states of performative boredom that elicited from him only new, increasingly arcane tasks for us. Unless you wanted to spend four hours of a Saturday polishing the TV aerial, or re-labelling paint cans, it was better to try to look busy. It was here that one of my dad's many moments of parenting genius proved mutually beneficial. He never told us to read; he had just built bookshelves in every room and filled them with a dazzling array of – mostly terrible – books, thereby ensuring that there would always be something to retreat to when boredom set in. And boredom – deep, crippling boredom – was pretty much a fixed state for a lot of my upbringing. I spent my childhood so bored, so paralytically intediated by my surroundings, that I found time to run through every bookshelf in our house until I went cross-eyed.

I read my brothers' archive of slim paperbacks featuring ladies in corsets holding pistols or ladies in metal bras wielding swords; sports capers with names like *GOAL!* or *NET!* or *HEADER!*, the plots of which invariably involved an oft-unused sub from a broken home coming on to score the decisive strike in a big final. There were also bizarrely highbrow works by Norman Mailer, Gore Vidal, Thomas Pynchon, and Stanisław Lem, but with no literary background I'm not sure that I was even aware that there was such a thing as a bad book. There were simply books I had read and those I hadn't. Early on I remember someone telling me that even if you read a book a week for your entire life, and lived for eighty years and change, your lifetime haul would still only be about four thousand. I set out to beat that number

My first loves were the Roald Dahl and Enid Blyton collections peppered through every room, and the *Reader's Digest* versions of popular classics. Later there came the bullet-stopping King and Barker novels that formed an early taste for horror and the macabre. After these, I began working my way through my older sisters' shelves full of Judy Blume, Francine Pascal and, latterly, Danielle Steele, Jackie Collins and Jilly Cooper. *Polo* would be my first introduction to the world of sex. At the tender age of eleven I was highly intrigued by Cooper's descriptions of posh people bonking while wearing tight white trousers and receiving very fancy fax-machine messages. But many of the books in the girls' rooms were propaganda they had been made to bring home from school. I have very strong memories of one book about a ballerina with an eating disorder, and another that was ostensibly a manual for teenage mothers but was actually written to scare young women into not being teenage mothers while also explicitly asserting that any form of contraception was evil. Catholic education required that girls fear the prospect of pregnancy above all things, while creating the perfect condition of ignorance which would result in just that. Having said that, none of my sisters ever became a teen-age mother.

In Caoimhe and Fionnuala's rooms I found slightly more varied material for the younger lady. I was particularly taken with girls' comics from this time: *Jackie, Bunty, Mandy & Judy*, and the majestically uneventful *Twinkle*. Arriving in from Mass and eating Sunday dinner, I'd find myself filled (figuratively) with the Holy Spirit and (literally) beef gravy, and get a few pages in before full-bellied sleep would grab me for an hour or so in its downy claws. I'd wake up groggy and bloated, halfway through a particularly riveting edition of 'Nurse Nancy'.

Finally, I'd end up in my dad's room, stumbling through his airport potboilers. My dad was an avid reader, particularly of news and politics, but when it came to fiction he was a stolid supporter of the page-turner, and was rarely seen without a thriller of varying quality. He loves John Grisham, Tom Clancy, Patricia Cornwell and Robert Ludlum, and I have hazy memories of him reading template special-forces action thrillers that always had titles that seemed as though they were formed from random pairings of cool-sounding words, like *The*

Decagon Opprobrium Crisis, Diagnosis: Parabellum or *Midnight at the Prolepsis Confabulation.*

Since my father loved thrillers, and is a proud Catholic, I wondered if he'd take to Dan Brown's preposterous blasphemy puzzle book, *The Da Vinci Code.* We were all delighted to discover he loved it and was able to park his tribal affinity in favour of the Catholic hierarchy long enough to become absorbed in the book's mixture of Vatican intrigue and what amounted to a series of remedial word scrambles. He was especially enamoured of the book's trip through the machinations of Opus Dei, singled out by Dan Brown as the shadowy puppet-masters of the papacy, a diabolical cadre of spies, archivists and killer monks enlisted to keep the church's secrets through deception, intrigue and as few words as possible containing two or more syllables.

'It does make you think, you know,' he announced, incorrectly, to the sitting room one sleepy Sunday, licking a finger and turning a page with relish. Such was my father's fondness for this ripping yarn that his suspicions regarding Opus Dei remained undiminished even when we reminded him that it was the self-same organisation he'd been a member of since 1983. 'That's a different thing,' he said absent-mindedly, before returning to the bad anagrams and short sentences that had held the book-reading world in thrall. One should never, I presume, let facts get in the way of a good clergy.

9

Fame!

Much of my childhood was spent feeling starved of the attention I surely deserved. There being eleven of us meant we were all getting less direct adulation than most children, and then my mother was cruelly withdrawn for ever, cutting that already meagre ration in half. I should have realised this was a problem for each of my siblings, but in my head no one had it as bad as me. For one thing, I came late in the pack, arriving at a time when my parents were so used to small children that the lustre of yet one more was probably somewhat diffused. I figured this alone started me off with something of a handicap. My older siblings had enjoyed fractionally more attention, and for longer periods, as they had each constituted a greater overall percentage of the total stock until their immediate successor was born.

I began deploying a miser's arithmetic to gauge this shortfall. Were one to use this metric — and, baby, I invented it — then as the ninth child simple mathematical logic meant my relative attention stats were at near-critical levels. The fact that my two younger siblings must therefore have more parlous stats than me was not something I deemed noteworthy. At seven, I was tabulating a mental index that catalogued every second of favour my siblings got at my expense, every shred of attention, sympathy or recognition. What was most galling was the fact that I was undoubtedly the most interesting member of my family, and by a long way. Why was Daddy so endlessly fascinated by, say, Mairead's GCSEs or Maeve and Orla's summer trip to America, but not the fact I'd seen a very large pigeon outside? Why was he putting so much time and effort into helping Shane or Dara prepare for university abroad, and yet so unenthused by my big news that sixty-five million years ago the dinosaurs died out due to an asteroid impact in Mexico's Yucatán Peninsula?

I bristled at being ignored like this, since I thought I had a good shot at leading the clan. Look at the facts: I knew hundreds of jokes cribbed from at least eighteen joke books, I could draw Sonic the Hedgehog freehand, and I'd read my way through the entire house so could always recommend amazing reads for the whole family – and even where to dodge the rude bits in Jackie Collins novels, by volume and page number, in case anyone was bashful about such things. On the physical side, I could jump right over the fence as long as I used one hand, and could regularly get to one hundred keepie-uppies, twenty if someone was watching. I mean, I was putting together a pretty impressive portfolio here, and it was getting me nowhere.

Reluctantly, I came to realise it was better to compare myself to my immediate contemporaries, focusing on the attention Caoimhe, Fionnuala and Conall received from Daddy. As Wee Ones we were the shakings of the bag, leftover bits of excess batter that clung between the folds of newspaper from the chippy order. This placed us in a different category of interest, for everyone. Evidently the closer you got to adulthood, the more interesting you became; which, considering how uniformly boring teenagers and adults appeared to be, seemed like a joke, and not one of the gut-busters from Jerry Chmielewski's 1978 classic *Jerry's Joke Book: Crazy, Funny, Polish and other Ethnic Jokes*, which I had read from cover to cover, and from which I could recite if you cared to ask. Worse still, this arrangement wasn't merely unfair but wildly inefficient. I was the star player, sitting on the bench week after week. It was odd that life had designated me the sole protagonist of reality, then so wantonly wasted my talents

It was probably, I surmised, a bit like neglect, and I almost certainly had it worse than any child who had ever lived, even those ones standing up in dirty cots wearing ratty jumpers in the fundraising ads for foreign orphanages. At least they were on TV. For a few days at the end of 1993, however, I too would find my way to the silver screen, when our home hosted an RTÉ camera crew. I was eight, I was irresistible, and I was not going to let my chance get away from me. This was the best thing that had ever happened to me, as is confirmed by the essay I wrote about it the next day in school, entitled 'The Best Thing That Has Ever Happened to Me'. I was clearly at least marginally aware of how crass this might sound, so I began the essay with a little prologue, 'The Sad Part', which got the reader up to speed on the fact my mother had died, it was terrible, etc., etc. The meat of the thing was about how great it was that so tragic an event had led to me experiencing a few days as a screen star on Ireland's national broadcaster.

Did Ye Hear Mammy Died?

Family Matters was a programme that dealt, appropriately enough, with all kinds of matters pertaining to families. Really boring Irish families. It was presented by two couch-dwelling presenters in loud outfits, who would throw to pre-taped reports on 'issues' and then circle back to the couch for follow-ups. Segments would include short pieces on, say, the rising price of school dinners, followed by a curt interview, in the studio, with the minister for education, in which she would say it was sad that school dinners were so expensive, and she'd look into it. Another segment would be about the difficulties of balancing work and home life, a topic illustrated with the story of a family in Roscommon that had to balance the demands of their llama farm with the extracurricular rigmarole of their kids' passion for stilt-walking. They also did very worthy segments about tragic things that happened to families, and it was under this remit we were recommended, I presume by someone in Derry who had run out of friends to tell about our awful misfortune and fancied spreading the news further still. The word reached my father that RTÉ were interested, but he was reluctant, not least since this wasn't the first time the media had come looking for an angle, and the previous occasion had not gone well.

In July 1992 we were featured in *Take a Break*, a weekly women's magazine that specialised – in fact still specialises – in tacky and exploitative coverage of human-interest stories. *Take a Break* touts itself as 'Britain's bestselling women's weekly' and it has, if anything, become odder since we were in it. 'I dug up my fella's secret lover INSIDE OUR HOUSE', and 'DEMON STRUCK as we PEELED POTATOES' being two recent examples of cover stories. To make the whole effect even more queasy, each cover features a smiling woman who is not a celebrity or the subject of any of the stories featured, but rather a model they've hired to fill space that would otherwise be blank. I am moderately obsessed with these women and the function they perform. *Take a Break* know what they're doing, so there must be a reason why she's there. Presumably their research shows that people are so used to seeing smiling women on magazine covers that it simply doesn't matter if the person in question is uncoupled from all of the horror and insanity around her. The cover woman is some form of basic avatar with whom the reader can identify. Self-possessed, sunny, aspirationally pretty but not unrelatably so, and nearly always turning to look lovingly outward, promising you, dear reader, that buying this magazine could make you stare delightedly at strangers, just like she does. Her bright clothes and wide smile are drastically at odds with the macabre and unsettling messaging around her. She creates the impression that this reader's friend is herself the person to whom these stories refer, and is thus the woman whose 'cruel hubby STUFFED a dying girl into a SUITCASE', or had ended up, oh cruellest of fates, 'PREGNANT by MOSQUITOES'. Therein lies the magazine's timeless appeal for those who love sensationalism and schmaltz, or just something sufficiently unhinged that it might take their mind off an impending root canal as they sit in a dentist's waiting room.

In our case, we were very much the other type of story that the magazine offers: maudlin tales of adversity that just about approximate real events. These remove every scintilla of complexity and nuance from a person's life story and mulch the whole thing into a frictionless pap digestible by any reader, no matter how unbothered by detail or distracted of mind. There was nothing here that would demand more than 3 per cent of the brain power God gave a tapeworm. I imagine the hope among the editorial team was that they could one day write a story so blandly, effortlessly readable that its broadest details could be gleaned by someone who'd just been kicked in the head by a horse. This they did with the story of my mother's death, under the sickly-sweet headline 'For the Love of MUM'.

'Gripping her husband Joe's hand, Sheila O'Reilly pulled him close. "Promise me you'll look after the children. Bring them up so I'd be proud," she said.'

My mother had, of course, never said anything of the sort, or at least Daddy had never mentioned it, perhaps out of a fear it would ruin our perception of her as someone who spoke to people in the way human beings generally do. The problems, alas, were not limited to those of taste, but of mind-boggling inaccuracy. *Take a Break* gave my mother's job as marriage counsellor, when she was a teacher. They quoted us referring to her as 'Ma', 'Mum' and 'Mummy', which impressively enough were all terms for Mammy that we would never have used in a million years. 'Ma' in particular seemed like an insulting flash of improvisation that suggested our English correspondent imagined us speaking with a catch-all Oirish lilt, some way north of Darby O'Gill. They misspelled three of our names and forgot about Shane entirely. Most impressive of all, however, was the following passage:

As Joe fell into a troubled sleep in bedroom number two of the bungalow, the children were still awake. Maeve and Orla, the identical twins, had their heads together. 'Sinead's doing three A-levels,' said Maeve. 'She won't have much time.' 'And Dara's in the middle of his GCSEs,' added Orla. 'The others are too young,' said Maeve. One by one they ticked off their brothers and sisters. The solution was simple. 'That leaves us,' they agreed. They waited until dawn, climbed out of bed and got dressed.

When Joe came down the stairs the next morning he stood still in the hallway and stared into the kitchen, blinking in astonishment. The place was spotless, the breakfast things neatly laid out. 'Hey, and what's this?' he asked, eyeing a chart on the wall.

'That's the rota,' chorused Maeve and Orla. 'We've worked it out. Sinead and Dara are excused as much as possible because of their exams.' Joe ran his eye down the list; dishwashing, dusting, vacuuming, and laundry. The twins had thought of everything.

This short segment contains so many painfully notable moments it's hard to know where to start. For one thing, my father and sisters seem to be communicating through the kind of expositional dialogue that suggests they've just been parachuted into their own lives and need to take stock of things and people they've known intimately for, in my sisters' case, their whole lives. For another, unless confined to prison or on an oil rig, human beings generally don't sleep in numbered bedrooms.

But what is possibly most notable about this passage is something you might not even have caught. The writer managed to describe the first bungalow in the history of architecture to possess a set of stairs.

The factual points were, of course, entirely secondary to the tone and style of the thing, which left such an acrid taste in our mouths that even now, thirty years later, it makes us angry. It was grisly to think of other people reading this mawkish bollocks and taking it as some true statement about our lives. It seemed inhuman that they were even allowed to turn our story into a tawdry bit of sentimental fluff for people to tut along to and say how sad. It's a fear I entertain myself whenever I ask my family for details of this or that part of my life story, since it is invariably a part of theirs too. None of this dissuaded my dad from taking part in *Family Matters*, though, perhaps because RTÉ were a much more respectable outlet, or maybe just because the presence of cameras would make it harder for them to lie about us having stairs.

At the time, it didn't seem strange that a TV show was coming to tell the story of my family's bereavement. It's surreal to think that, conservatively, tens of thousands of people must have watched a segment about my home life, and we all just went about our business afterwards. I can see that our story was sufficiently family-focused to fit on a show that was primarily about family matters, but I find it hard to work out why such a show existed in the first place. I've never seen anything since with a remit that uninspiringly specific. Everyone has a family, the logic may have gone, so let's create this oddly stilted, low-stakes parish newsletter television programme that was like a busybody bulletin board for parents around the country and a platform for people to complain about the frustrations of family life. It was a bit like *Crimewatch*, if the only crimes they covered were people charging too much for textbooks, bad parking near playgrounds and the hassle of school uniforms going tatty after a couple of washes.

None of this mattered to me at the time since, as far as I was concerned, I had pretty much been cast as the lead in a new *Die Hard* film. The crew descended at some point in December 1993 and I quickly made a nuisance of myself. You can see it was December because, even though the show was eventually broadcast in the spring, the footage clearly shows our Christmas decorations everywhere. This became an oddly persistent point of reference for anyone who would later see the show. 'Saw your Christmas decorations there, in the background!' they'd say, in a tone that suggested they'd foiled our cunning ruse. 'Yes, it was filmed at Christmas,' we'd say, never really shaking the sense that they considered us very neatly caught out. The crew were in our house for about eight hours over two days, and the premise of the segment was simple enough; my dad and my eldest sister Sinead spoke to camera about my mother's illness and death, and then Maeve and Orla discussed their famous rota, which had made them stars of print and now made its TV debut.

It should be stressed just how much celebrity this con-ferred upon them. Their teacher nominated them for a Young Citizen's Award, which they won, and which eventually saw them travel to London for the presentation. There, alongside people who'd raised money for epilepsy drugs or rescued dogs from disused mines, they attended a lavish ceremony and even got to meet Northern Irish funnyman Frank Carson, a fixture on local TV during the exact period of time when comedians still went by 'funnyman' in the tabloids.

It was undoubtedly true that Maeve and Orla took on a huge amount of work themselves when they really were too young to do so. For this, they received praise from teachers – and TV funnymen – but also near-constant ribbing from their siblings, who quite unfairly discerned in their efforts a certain self-importance.

Because we were (and still are) a mercilessly sarcastic shower of cynics, for years afterwards their award became a byword for deluded self-congratulation and was recalled exclusively in mocking tones. This ignored the fact that, eight weeks after our mother's death, they spent the run-up to Christmas making trips out to the caravan in our back garden, scouring Argos catalogues so they could source and collect all of our Christmas presents. They'd worked out Santa wasn't real only the year before, meaning they had, in some sense, lost Santa and Mammy within twelve months, and were now being asked to perform some of the functions of both. Looking back now, it seems odd that this job fell to two eleven-year-olds, considering a fifteen-year-old, a sixteen-year-old and an eighteen-year-old were also available, but the logic behind it was never really explained to me. It was said that the older kids were too focused on exams, but the few weeks before Christmas aren't exactly fever pitch for scholastic activities. In any case, the twins did it. And, in return, we teased them for decades afterwards.

While the film crew, like everyone else, centred their focus on my older siblings, I made myself busy behind the scenes, picking up cables and peering through cameras in a way that suggested this was my fourth shoot this week, but with a punctilious edge that implied I thought standards were slipping. I would repeat things I heard them say, as if I too thought we needed a brighter lamp for the kitchen shots, and had myself just been thinking they needed to hurry up with the externals before evening set in. When they started keeping their conversations, and equipment, away from me, I brought out the big guns: telling tantalising dinosaur facts just within earshot of those crew members who seemed the most discerning, hoping to bait them into asking for the full experience.

'Hey kid,' I imagined they'd shout, lowering a boom mic so as to focus more intently, 'what was that you were saying about the wingspan of a pterosaur?' This never came to pass. I eventually gained better access by going straight to the top and shadowing the producer, Marion. I think I can say she would have been completely lost had it not been for the guided tour of the house I offered, entirely free of charge, listing every room and its contents in a detailed but efficient way, giving her the basics of each in well under forty minutes. She must have found my incessant questions very enlightening, since she seemed anxious to get through as many of them as she could as quickly as possible, and was always telling me how little time she had. I was particularly interested in what, exactly, a producer did (many things), how many things she'd produced (plenty) and if a producer was more important than the director (they were, according to Marion). I also wanted to know if she had one of those director's chairs, and if it was called a producer's chair, and if I could have one, and if she'd ever filmed a volcano, or in space, or if this would be shown in America, and if she had ever been to America, and if I should go to America to maximise my potential as a TV star. She let me wear headphones and look at the notes for the production, and showed me other tips and tricks of the trade. It was the first time I'd ever seen that 'let's wrap this up' gesture TV people use for segments that are going on too long, when she made one towards a cameraman as a way of telling him to stop letting me look through the viewfinder for the eightieth time that day.

It was exciting to have these people in our house, but also mildly unnerving. Occasionally, I'd be aware of them moving something, a pot or a fruit bowl, so it wouldn't be in frame. This was probably just so the viewer's eye wouldn't be distracted by something in the background, but I took it to be a judgement on the feng shui of our home, as if it were unimaginably gauche to have a fruit bowl on a countertop when it was so better suited to being on the table instead. I made mental notes of their decisions and for years afterwards would unconsciously make these same adjustments if I passed, say, a cup that was too close to the television, or three chairs packed tightly together when it would be more aesthetically pleasing for them to be ever so slightly spaced out.

In reality, I guess they tiptoed around me because our story really was that sad, and they were probably very moved, if not moderately freaked out, by how excited I was to be part of all of this. They may also have been wondering just how best to get closer to this marvellous young man who surely had such a huge career ahead of him; to nurture his genius, or maybe hang on to his coat tails and follow him to fame and fortune. I expected immediate stardom and requests for paid work doing public appearances; opening youth centres, doing in-store events at shopping malls, that kind of thing. I imagined myself being charming and precocious on late-night chat shows and studiously refusing to mention my siblings unless they were extra nice to me in the days beforehand.

All I wanted was to be something like a low-level god, pampered in easy wealth and adored by everyone I met. Like most children, I had watched the careers of child actors like Macaulay Culkin and Mara Wilson and seen a template I wanted to pursue for myself. I had little to no interest in, nor aptitude for, anything in the dramatic line. It's just that unlike, say, medicine or international finance, acting seemed like something for which children could be famous. I figured I'd just sort out the work side of the deal later, while keeping the fame and fortune part as my guiding light. Besides, it seemed obvious that most child actors weren't particularly good, so I could leverage my appeal on my amazing personality and all this wisdom I was picking up about shot choices, light rigs and cup placement.

I barely made an appearance in the eight-minute final cut. I was in a few group shots, and one heavily staged sequence in which we were filmed walking out of our front door on the way to school. As I've said, no one used the front door of our house except visiting priests or doorknockers, so this had a perverse ring of falsity I found incredibly thrilling. Here we were, acting. As ourselves, of course, but acting nonetheless. This brief walk to school in our uniforms – donned on a day when we weren't even in school – struck a note of duplicity I found so exciting I reckoned I would never get tired of it, no matter how many BAFTAs I won. Unfortunately, my only other appearance of note was the one for which the show became notorious to all who watched it, in our family and out: a lamentable sequence in which Conall and I are shown kicking a ball around the garden. This wouldn't have been too bad, except a combination of factors made it seem like a home movie shot in Chernobyl. For one thing, it was a particularly dismal December day – like I told the crew, shot choices are everything when you're chasing the light – so both Conall and I were suffused with a grainy, greyish tinge. On top of that, we were wearing scuffed-up little dress shoes that suggested we probably didn't have trainers, most likely because none had been dropped into our garden that week by a NATO helicopter. Lastly, there was the fact that it was not a football we were kicking, but a rugby ball, entirely deflated. This we paddled toward each other while attempting not to gurn at the camera, giving us the gormless effect of two rain-soaked peasant children taking a break from our labours by cheerily kicking an oblong leather bag filled with potato peel. It seemed as though a factory horn might at any moment call us back in for eight more hours at the smelting plant.

Friends of my father were quick to point out that we had been captured drinking out of mugs with no handles, and that a poem written by Caoimhe had been inelegantly fixed to the wall with masking tape rather than the more classy Blu Tack. These were, it must be understood, merely those comments they made to our faces. Lord knows what people said among themselves.

Watching it back now, twenty-five years later, I'm surprised we were so embarrassed since it was handled with a great deal more sensitivity than memory allows. The hosts were sympathetic and serious, and my dad conducted himself with incredible dignity and eloquence, not least when he described breaking down upon seeing my mother's dead body for the first time. He's remarkably comfortable in front of camera – my Hollywood biographers will likely say that's where I got it from – and is incredibly moving in conversation, even maintaining his composure as he describes leaving the hospital room where she lay and re-entering it again on the off chance that something, somehow, would be different when he returned. These were memories I can't remember him sharing, probably because I was too young to understand them. By the time I was old enough, the tape of the show had become an object of fear and horror in our house. Not because of the feelings evoked by his thoughtful words, but because we couldn't bear to see ourselves portrayed as somehow poor or pitiful.

The eight-minute segment was part of an episode that was mostly taken up with a piece lamenting the price of schoolbooks. Our part done, we watched as the show moved on. A series of statistics were read out about just how massively the price of these books had increased in a few short years. A minister came on afterwards, declaring that the situation was indeed something that gave her grave concern, and said she would look into it.

10

Jeremy

I'm often asked, if my mother had survived, would my parents have gone on to have more children? I'm reluctant to say no, since I'm sure every last one of my parents' friends lost good money betting any of the first ten would be the end of it. On the other hand, maybe it's for the best that they stopped when they did, since our minibus only held thirteen, and strapping children to the roof wouldn't have done for long journeys. Certainly not the longest trip we ever took as a family, one considered so perilous that my father arranged the blessing of the caravan. With God's good grace on our side, we set off in the big white minibus for Spain to visit Aileen, my mother's sister, pulling the caravan behind us.

The blessing was probably a good idea, since after a few years of steady service the wheels had actually come off the old caravan. Daddy had been driving it home when the reassuringly steady *flump-a-dump* behind him morphed into an altogether less reassuring metallic shriek, followed by an angle-grinder's flurry of sparks, forcing an immediate abandonment of his now decidedly less mobile cargo in a field just outside St Johnston. The ABI Award Superstar we got in its place was much larger, extending our full bus and trailer length to over forty feet, just the thing you want for a 3400-mile round trip taking in all of France, the Pyrenees, a coast-hugging jaunt across Spain's northern shores, and then back again.

Carting eleven children across Europe by road would be difficult in most circumstances, but doing so in a minibus dragging a huge caravan while coming off the back of a serious bereavement is a frankly insane proposition. We had travelled before, but not much lately, and maybe it was this urge for a change of scenery that drove my father to make the trip – that, and a sense of giving us something to look forward to, to make us feel excited and happy and young.

We were making the trip without Sinead, who was recovering from appendicitis and would follow us on. My eldest brothers, Shane and Dara, sat up front next to my dad. Behind that there was one bank of four seats, another bank of three, and then two banks of two at the very back where the four Wee Ones sat facing each other, in the manner of one of those drop helicopters you see in action movies. I say four, but there were really five of us, since we were joined on this jaunt by a special guest, Conall's imaginary friend, Jeremy.

Jeremy had appeared a few months earlier, almost always in the context of any child-height mischief for which Conall, the baby of the family at three years old, was being blamed. Jeremy had eaten scones that were left out. Jeremy had stood on the dog's tail. Jeremy had stolen the contents of a coin dish in my godmother's house and placed them in Conall's tiny little trouser pockets so that he jangled when he walked bow-legged out to the car like a penguin who'd shat himself. Jeremy's presence was so fascinating that we didn't so much tolerate as support and promote the idea of him wholeheartedly. None of us had any experience of seeing someone interact with an imaginary friend, and it turned out to be enormously entertaining. It also seemed to embolden Conall to do naughty things, which was always fun to watch, and even more so when he got caught and would insist – enraged – that 'Germany did it'. Conall was one of the few people unlucky enough to have acquired an imaginary friend whose name he couldn't pronounce.

Our father manned the cassette player, and the soundtrack included Irish Dad classics like Christy Moore, ABBA, Clannad and Planxty, supplemented by odder touchstones like the Carpenters' back catalogue and, weirdly, the original cast recordings for *Chess* and *Cats*. These we would listen to on repeat until he could be talked into ceding control to Dara, who, due to his place in the passenger seat, could occasionally throw on U2, REM or the Housemartins. I can't think of those long trips in the minibus without hearing the strains of 'Memory' sung by Elaine Page, or the Carpenters' 'Superstar', borne on the blue-grey wisps of cigar smoke that emanated from the driver's seat for the entire journey.

The smoke was a constant of my childhood. Aside from a brief break in the late eighties, my father smoked several packs of Hamlet mid-sized cigars every day, until he finally gave up a few months before his fiftieth birthday in 1997. A rough cough caused him to take some time off work, which was entirely unprecedented. This clearly spooked him – missing work, I think, more than the sickness itself – and without any fanfare he quit his thirty-five-year habit and never had so much as a puff again. Back in 1992, however, the cigar smoke permeated every object in our house, and especially the fabric seats in the minibus. It's likely they also gave his eleven children a not unpleasant, woody aroma we probably couldn't smell off ourselves. This smell was only momentarily pleasant, however, since it quickly grew stale and acrid on everything it touched, which was, well, everything. This could also have been a contributor to the frequent, horrible bouts of car sickness which beset several of us, most especially Fionnuala and Dearbhaile, both so inclined to vomiting on road trips that travelling with them was as precarious as cycling through a minefield carrying a large, open vat of parmesan soup in your lap. I think Fionnuala's record was the time she was violently ill before we'd even reached the end of our drive. Even after wiping, bagging, cleaning and airing for a few minutes, it put a rather unsavoury pall over the next few hours' travel.

Having dragged ourselves to England, we drove south and boarded an overnight ferry from Portsmouth, itself a heady thrill. There was something so monumentally eventful about driving into the belly of a giant boat and climbing through its innards to a waiting bed. The clank of each step through the petrol fumes in the blindingly lit car hold, all the way up the twangy metallic stairs to the carpeted cabins. Cabins! This alone, the prospect of staying in the eight-by-four metal box with my older brother Shane, was as exciting as boarding a rocket ship to Saturn's moons.

Once we were on the boat, as so often seemed to be the case in my childhood, I was given much more autonomy than one might expect for a six-year-old. It was assumed that wherever one of us wandered, we'd always be in sight of one or other sibling. Dara, who was sixteen, spent most of the time trying to get served at the bar, or peeling off for cheeky smokes in the face of hurricane-speed winds on the deck. My joy was to check out the labyrinthine ball pit and the ferry's cavernous arcades. I dread to think how small and depressing these would seem to my older eyes, how damp and sad and, doubtless, riddled with germs. But, at the time, this was heaven itself. I was fascinated by the arcade games, *Double Dragon*, *Metal Slug* and *Streets of Rage*, blaring their screens and flashing their lights in attract mode, that half-state of activity that is an irresistible draw for impressionable kids. I'd happily jump on the console and bash away at buttons, unaware that I was having no effect whatsoever on the things happening on screen, or that money was required for it to happen.

I don't know what Daddy was going through on this journey. I can hardly imagine. Was he wearing the haunted look of someone so awfully bereaved, now carting ten minors on a 1700-mile journey across a continent? Or was he just getting on with it, as usual, letting the constant stream of small jobs keep him going? I barely gave it a second thought, so excited to be on ferries and in foreign supermarkets and then, oh bliss itself, arriving at the French campsites where we would stop at night and hear unfamiliar birds and even more unfamiliar speech from those around us. I was too young to care about playing the massive, forty-a-side football matches that my older brothers were using to make friends, so I contented myself with exploring the site for beetles or caterpillars I could poke and prod, on one occasion finding a particularly great stag beetle that I carried around on a stick to show other holidaying children, none of whom spoke English.

'Look,' I said, but slowly, in the hope this would allow them to overcome their stubborn refusal to recognise English words. Seeing that this was working, I shook the stick in a manner that conveyed, quite clearly, the meaning 'You have admired my stag beetle, we are now friends.' They understood me and, like the beetle himself (obviously all beetles are boys), desired to join my gang. The beetle demonstrated his own fealty by gripping the stick I held out from my body like a holy object, and my new pals did the same by flanking me on all sides as we approached other small children with this, our great news: the beetle was here. A charming détente established itself among us, this multilingual cohort of nerds who had come together to look at this beetle and maybe touch its carapace, using that wordless universal language of making an 'o' with your mouth as you stroke a very cool insect. It was a touching reminder of the unifying nature of pointing at things and wondering what they are.

It's likely that I got these dauntless communication skills from Daddy, who has always evinced a strange confidence in his ability to be understood in other languages, despite not speaking any other languages. He was no academic slouch, but was of a more mathematical bent, although his schooling had taught him a smattering of Greek, Latin and Irish. But he has the curious and endearing trait of presuming he's very good at most things until precisely the moment it is proven he isn't, at which point he will politely pretend he never tried in the first place.

He once insisted that he could 'probably speak most European languages', due to that aforementioned Latin and Greek he'd learned some forty years previously. 'You'll notice,' he offered, 'that most Spanish words are very much like English words, but with o on the end, and so on.' It's tempting to examine just how much heavy lifting 'and so on' is performing in that sentence, but suffice to say when we quizzed him for a moderate length of time he conceded that he may have simplified the concept of language acquisition just a tad. When words failed him, he subscribed to the Basil Fawlty method of speaking in English, but with a foreign accent

It's likely he had got away with this when travelling with my mother. In much the same way that, taken together, Usain Bolt and I have eight Olympic gold medals, I think proximity to her talent had given him a false sense of the worth of his own contributions to their linguistic interactions. Mammy was fluent in Irish and French, both of which she taught at A level, and she consumed novels and poetry in both languages. In her twenties, she taught herself rudimentary Spanish using only a phrasebook and non-stop badgering of Eduardo, her sister Aileen's Spanish husband. When she was entering her forties, my oldest siblings began studying German, and she decided she would start learning the language as well, doing night classes so she could keep up with their efforts. This, more than any-thing, epitomises my mother's best qualities; not merely endless compassion and thoughtfulness, but a work ethic that makes my head hurt. The kind of woman who, while balancing the demands of eleven kids and a full-time teaching job, decided to do a German GCSE from scratch. At night. Simply for the joy that it would bring her, and the service it could provide for her kids. The fact she earned a higher mark than Sinead at the end of the year was unremarked upon.

Jeremy

Irish was undoubtedly her best language, but her French was supposedly so good that she spoke it like a native, enabling us to holiday in more secluded, and likely cheaper, parts of France. In 1988, we spent two weeks in a farmhouse in Pont-Aven, for which I was too young to remember much more than it being the time my father had first quit smoking. That and seas of yellow fields, terracotta tiles and a delightfully ramshackle old tractor that sat by one of the barns behind the house. A little while into the holiday, Mammy became withdrawn and reserved, and spent at least one full day by herself in her room. My mother was usually so calm and sunny that for her to entirely shield herself from view was as absurd as it would have been to see her sumo wrestling. A glance at the calendar suggests this was the day she found the lump that heralded the second recurrence of her cancer, and which two months later would cause her to have a mastectomy. The following day she was just as lively and together as before, focusing on the positive, determined to get on with things. Daddy started smoking again.

When his own stock of phrases ran out, my father delegated all communication to those whose language skills surpassed his own. When it came to French, this meant Maeve and Orla. At twelve, they had a single year of secondary-school French, making them capable of indicating numbers of things and naming basic household objects and activities. Daddy deemed this sufficient for the twins to do most of the talking, not just to shopkeepers or rural folk we'd ask for directions, but to campsite officials, border guards and police. A significant communication gap persisted throughout the French portion of our excursion, taking us through long stretches of arid, yellow-brown countryside populated entirely by people with no interest in Maeve and Orla's favourite colours, pets or subjects in school.

We entertained ourselves on the road by singing hymns and popular hits, usually en masse. We were raised to think it was perfectly normal, in fact desirable, to break into collective song at the drop of a plectrum, but I can't help picturing what we looked like to other motorists as we hurtled past. Ten scrubbed little faces, silently belting out 'How Great Thou Art', their eyes closing for the high notes as they careened down the autoroute.

For the Wee Ones in the back, our time was spent either giddily demented or bored out of our minds. Unfortunately, these swings rarely synced up, so at least one of us was elated and another seething with contemptuous boredom at all times. Add to that Conall's constant quest to keep Jeremy under control, and Fionnuala desperately trying to stop her stomach from becoming an external organ, and we were an eventful little cohort of activity, albeit one studiously ignored by everyone else for the entire five days of our journey.

We stayed sane by playing interminable bouts of I spy, which began as nothing more than a way to distract Fionnuala from being extravagantly sick every eight miles, but soon became wildly competitive. Caoimhe and I led the charge as the two oldest Wee Ones, and became increasingly creative. We quickly set upon the fact that if we said 'I spy with my little eye, something beginning with . . . A' we could subvert the natural order of the game by using a in its indefinite-article sense, as in 'a car', 'a sheep', etc., which managed to frustrate any older players who'd occasionally take part. More frustrating still was

Conall's habit of picking the same three words – road, car, Jeremy – but refusing to admit it because it would mean his turn would be over.

'I spy,' he'd say, barely concealing his glee, 'with my little eye, something beginning with R.'

'R? Road?'

'No.'

'Conall, it's road again, isn't it?'

'No.'

'Conall, stop laughing. You'd tell us if it was road, wouldn't you?'

'...'

'Conall.'

'Yes, it's road.'

Looking back, I can see he was just delighted to have our full attention for a moment or two because I'm sure it was a rare enough occurrence for the three-year-old baby in a family of eleven. But, at the time, we wanted to throw him out the window.

The attention-seekers among us could break up the tedium by reflecting on the minor celebrity status we enjoyed. We caused a sensation wherever we stopped, since the sight of all ten of us – Jeremy being invisible, even to French toddlers – crowded inside the minibus was too fascinating for many passers-by to resist. We routinely caught kids pressing their noses up against their windows in astonishment, or people counting us out of the minibus with their fingers or coming over to my father and asking him, in French, if these children were really all his own. The effect was even more pronounced in Lourdes, where people associated having a large family with a certain godliness. Occasionally, words were abandoned and they simply shook my father by the hand, as if he had just heroically rescued us from a house fire.

For the older kids, I presume this was a little embarrassing, but I thought it was great, and would probably have set down a little cloth cap and sung 'Danny Boy' for a few francs had the chance arisen. It was enjoyable to be an object of fascination, even if there was a not-too-small kernel of pity to people's interest. In any case, if it was my wish to be stared at, then that wish came true many times. Not least when, a mile from our campsite in San Sebastian, as we were driving at high speed, the sliding door of the minibus fell off and clattered to the ground.

To this day, my father denies that this suggests any problem with the bus and blames his feckless children for the entire thing. 'Yous didn't close it right,' was what he said then about the door, and it is a mantra he still repeats, over a quarter century later. I'm personally of the opinion that there should not exist a method of closing a vehicle's door, no matter how careless, that would precipitate it being ejected from said vehicle several hours later, at seventy miles an hour. But such observations fall on deaf ears. Joe O'Reilly is a wonderful man, and a doting father, but he will often side with mechanical objects over his children. If it comes down to a dispute between one of us and a six-foot metal door panel clunking to the ground in a shower of sparks, he'll take the door's word for it every time.

We stopped to survey the damage, and Daddy, Shane and Dara retrieved the hulking door, which appeared still intact. They gingerly reconnected it on its rollers but, not trusting it to remain there, we drove the rest of the way to the campsite at a crawl, with Shane and Dara jogging alongside holding the door from without, like secret service agents escorting a world leader who had been reduced to travelling to a G8 summit in a minibus with caravan attached, via a two-star campsite in the Basque Country. God knows what the people who ran the campsite made of us as we turned the corner and entered their premises in a minibus held together with holy water, grease and the outstretched palms of two adolescent boys. We might as well have entered in a giant parping clown car with a big rubber horn, a backfiring exhaust pipe and Granny O'Reilly strapped to the roof in her rocking chair, firing off six-shooters to announce our arrival.

Daddy was able to mend the door, and we were able to continue our journey in this decidedly blessed conveyance – albeit after a strict lecture regarding the procedure for its opening and closing. We arrived in Galicia the following day. Once we were in La Coruña, we had two weeks of sun-dappled splendour with Aileen and family, tripping to the sea, sampling exotic local produce and eating them out of house and home. Aileen and Eduardo's own sons, Jaime and Juan, had already left for university by this time, but returned for our visit, meaning my aunt and uncle went from having two people in the house to sixteen. Spain seemed idyllic – warm, relaxed and filled with inordinately pleasing local details that appeared to have been cribbed from a reductive and xenophobic cartoon: the daily siestas that saw old men snoring loudly from nearby balconies; even older ladies in spotted dresses who seemed to spend all their time shooing dogs and beating rugs against low walls.

God knows how Aileen was able to entertain us all that time, but she managed, with the heavily gendered result that the girls had shopping trips and the boys had football outings. No O'Reilly holiday would be complete without checking in on the interred remains of one of Christ's apostles – in this case James, son of Zebedee – so we also did a day trip to the cathedral at Santiago de Compostela. I remember eating paella, and push-pop ice lollies which we didn't yet have in Ireland, and tasting squid for the first time, deep fried, and loving it above all things, most especially since I could make out its little eyes and legs and felt pleasingly giant as a result. I remember the Barcelona Olympics were going on at the time, giving me a pleasant sense of being right at the centre of the world. Never mind it was taking place over five hundred miles away, so that, despite having travelled seventeen hundred miles to get to La Coruña, we were actually only four hundred miles closer to Barcelona than we had been in Derry. It *felt* as though I was there.

Daddy spent a lot of time with Aileen, speaking, I imagine, of the wife and sister they'd lost. I realise now that they were experiencing grief at different speeds. Aileen had had more time and space to reflect on and mourn her sister's passing, while Daddy had obviously been kept busy with the daily demands of a full-time job and eleven children. More than most, Aileen understood how difficult all of this was going to be for us in the long run, and I think she suspected Daddy was still in shock. She knew for a fact that his children were, and the smallest of us particularly. Conall had circled the wake asking when Mammy was coming back, and still posed this question from time to time. Auntie Aileen was used to these kinds of queries, not least since she had been one of the people I'd confronted with my now famous death announcement, although my rendition for her had been a tad more bespoke. Having arrived at the house a little while later than everyone else, she found me in my parents' bedroom.

'Auntie Aileen,' I said gravely, 'I have some very bad news for you.'

'Have you?' she ventured.

'Mammy's dead,' I said, with a solemnity that would have been slightly more impactful had I not been bouncing up and down on the bed. 'If you want to see her, she's in the dining room,' I added helpfully, punctuating this sombre death notice with a commemorative belly flop.

La Coruña gave us respite from the tedium of life in Derry in a place where the weather and the people were sunny and bright. Perhaps the most striking moment of fame throughout the trip was when we sang in the local church, like some sort of visiting youth group of mourning Irish children. As with so many of our public outings, I have no idea how this came to pass, save that any thought that it was spontaneous is slightly undone by the clear memory I have of my father getting us there an hour early so he could bolt together the microphone stands he'd brought with us.

This is an aspect of my father that might surprise you, were you ever to meet him. He's a quiet and unassuming man, with a kindly smile and a very relaxed view on life. He doesn't look like the type of person who'd bring musical instruments, microphones and mic stands nearly two thousand miles from Ireland to Spain so that we could sing to a churchful of strangers. That my father did this – packed a twenty-six-foot caravan with the clothes, food, tents and miscellaneous luggage of ten children, while also making sure to include the equipment necessary for us to perform as a fully electric choir – didn't raise an eyebrow at the time. We went along with it, since singing at large Catholic gatherings was completely routine. Our performance ended with rapturous applause from the parishioners, and an uncomfortable impasse when it became clear they were blocking the route back to our seats, and thus impeding the exit that would signal for their applause to stop. They ended up clapping for what seemed like minutes, many of them in tears, not sure of when, or if, they would be permitted to stop. We thus continued standing there, like eleven little Stalins singing puzzlingly Christ-themed party songs at the Third International.

There were a few hiccups during the holiday, such as when all the gas in Auntie Aileen's house was switched off and a brief investigation revealed Jeremy to be the culprit. There was also the moment when I grabbed my Uncle Eduardo's reassuringly tanned hand on the beach, only to look up and discover it was not his hand at all, but that of another, quite alarmed, Spanish man, who recoiled from my clingy little grasp as if the see-through pallor of my Irish skin was infectious. But, for the most part, it was bliss, and we were as sad to leave as Aileen and Eduardo were, presumably, quietly relieved to have their house back to themselves.

Providence conspired to give our return trip a moderately memorable epilogue. As we approached Cherbourg, Conall cried, 'I can see the road!'

'Very good,' we replied.

'No, through the floor,' he clarified.

Jeremy

It was at this point we realised that the tow bar for the caravan had put so much strain on the minibus, it had wrenched a welt in the floor, right beneath where we were sitting. Unfortunately, it happened to be Bastille Day, so there were no garages open, and it seemed as though we were destined to spend a dismal day and night in the caravan, until we passed a farmhouse whose inhabitants, a family of eight, saw our distress and waved us in. Miraculously, they had everything we needed to fix the problem, not merely cutting tools and hammers, but steel and an oxy-acetylene torch. This last was wielded by the man of the house, the most French person I'd ever seen in my life, who performed the necessary welding with such nonchalance that the cigarette he smoked never left his bottom lip throughout. The lady of the house brought out lemonade, and Sinead thanked them all profusely in her best French, translating back to us their animated questions about the nature of our family, and their sincere commiserations upon hearing of our situation. She translated, too, their adamant refusals of any payment, which greatly pained my father until he remembered some Spanish brandy he had been gifted by a member of Aileen's church, which he himself would have little use for, and which he knew custom would bar them from refusing. They were much obliged, probably because they knew the value of it more than my father, who would subsequently discover it cost well over a hundred pounds. It was, I suppose, a small price to pay for getting us home in one piece.

Well, most of us. The trip home did precipitate one final departure. The Enya soundtrack, the cigar smoke, the constant, desultory rounds of I spy, all seemed lacking, since they were leading us away, and not toward, some greater destination.

Where the journey *over* had been suffused with a constant, gladdening fizz of anticipation, there was now a sense that summer was moulting layers of fun, and all enjoyment in the universe was creeping toward its natural end.

Perhaps it was this disaffection that led us to decree that Jeremy must not return to Ireland with us. In a short court proceeding held in the minibus just before we boarded the ferry, he was sentenced to death by a jury of his peers. He was seized and held by Shane, who said a few words before hoisting him half out the sliding window and then slamming it shut, cutting him in two and spraying his guts across the French countryside.

Conall wailed. We all regretted it immediately, more so when it became clear that our baby brother accepted Jeremy's demise as final and definite. Afterwards, he never once pretended Jeremy had survived. He had been real and alive, and Conall had watched him die. The bubble, like Jeremy's torso, had been burst. And Conall never again asked when someone dead would be coming back.

11

The Grand North Atlantic Home-Taped VHS Archive

Fearghal's dad had a poitín still, made from corrugated iron and covered in moss so you could only get at it from the one end. The cops didn't bother with it since they had bigger things to worry about than Denis's homebrew hooch, and the craggy hill that traced up from Termonbacca and out toward Creggan was uncharted land to them and their armoured cars. Ferghal's dad was awful fond of talking about the still, its contents and the arcane processes of the trade, not to mention the near misses with vandals and smugglers, tussles with neighbours, or the odd bedraggled fox that might pad through the scrub toward the sweet-smelling, foul-smelling vats. No trip to Ferghal's house was complete without Denis telling some tall tale about his rough and roguish secret life as a contrabandist. The great joy of Denis's life was when someone gagged, uncontrollably, at the mucky liquid he'd scraped from the still that week. One sniff and it was promised you'd go blind, two and you could read people's thoughts for a fortnight. A drop on your tongue and we reckoned you'd speak six words to the dead, then die. Denis was the sort of low-level eccentric who prevailed throughout my childhood, men who seemed completely normal until you had a conversation with them about planning permission or female newsreaders and found that their many and varied eccentricities would foam to the surface, fully realised.

For Percy's dad, Pat, it was spoons. He collected spoons from every place he ever visited, and took to delegating the procurement of these blessed objects to anyone going anywhere, as if they were a tribute owed. Many a conversation was halted by Pat nudging his head in the direction of his spoon box and asking had you anything in your pocket for him.

Compared to such foibles and fancies, my dad's own hobbies seemed slightly less niche. He had no interest in sport, save a passion for Formula One that alienated and intrigued me in equal measure. He loved cars and racing from a purely technical standpoint, and was subsumed by the drama of every tune, stop and corner. I tend to share the sentiment of Sean Lock when it comes to Formula One, in that I would get the same amount of enjoyment from turning on two washing machines at the same time and seeing which finished first. What makes Sean Lock's gag even more applicable here is that my dad genuinely would, and I think at least once actually did, enjoy watching two washing machines go at once. We had two right beside each other in our utility room – the prison laundry – and routine testing of their abilities would have been par for the course.

When we were growing up, Daddy liked nothing more than lying, supine, on a grubby cloth he'd laid on the floor, muttering the names of screws to himself while he tried to 'fix' a machine he'd bought that same day. Our garage is still a mausoleum of bikes, mowers and machines of all types and stripes. My dad is not exactly a hoarder, but he does still maintain that the six old Superser heaters he has there will likely come in handy some time soon. Ditto the four or five propeller mowers, two or three ride-on tractor mowers, and a thousand other units of mechanical detritus that have sat in our cavernous garage for so long you could spend a lifetime there and never notice them.

This gadget graveyard was useful to us as kids, in the sense that it occasionally sucked Daddy into a time warp that gave us free rein for a few hours, especially on Saturdays, when he would otherwise be lining up chores for us. So when he was preoccupied, it was glorious. We'd watch him head out to the garage, intending to find, say, a pair of pliers, or a photograph of John Paul II, and audibly cheer as we watched him get waylaid mending a strimmer that hadn't seen active use in twenty-two years. As we got older, we'd sometimes seed these distractions ourselves.

'We don't have a chainsaw, do we, Daddy?' I'd ask innocently.

'Why?' he'd reply.

'Oh, it's nothing. Well, Kev Nash said he didn't believe that we had a chainsaw, not one that worked anyway.'

'Did he now?' This with indignation. 'Well, would he be surprised to know that we actually have three?'

'But working, I mean.'

'They work fine,' he'd retort, putting on his jacket and

reaching for the garage door remote as my siblings and I prepared a mental schedule of which terrible action movies we'd
be watching in the sitting room in eighteen seconds' time.

This was only good, of course, as long as he didn't press-
gang you into service, which was a very real threat. That was
the worst of all possible worlds, worse even than being given
typical Saturday-morning Daddy jobs like fixing the gutters or
hoeing the weeds. Those, at least, were drawn from our own
dimension of time and space, chores with purpose and an end.
Hoking around in the garage with Daddy, by contrast, was a
senseless infinity of thankless tasks. It meant at least an hour
of Daddy barking orders at you to hand him invisible, often
impossible, objects, which he described solely in relation to
their proximity to other impossible objects you were supposedly standing beside.

'Pass me the goblin fork,' he'd shout. 'The goblin fork! The
red one. With the ladle bells. The *ladle bells*. It's over there,
beside the cheese press – ach, for Jesus' sake it's right in front
of you!' He would then walk precisely to where you were
standing and materialise a gigantic object that somehow bore
all the unlikely characteristics he'd just mentioned, which had
been sitting right in front of you this entire time, sandwiched
between an inflatable pulpit, a bag of javelins and the Nepalese
Handball Federation's team bus. There were ham radios, pool
tables and plough parts. I'm fairly sure at one point we had a
large mechanical loom. Once I was instructed to find something behind 'the ship's engine'. This I did, even though my
father has never fished nor sailed in his life.

Daddy is an avid technophile. Perhaps this is an inherited
trait. During the fifties, his parents became the first people on

the street to have a television, which caused a great stir at the time, and led to neighbours and family members constantly dropping in to catch whatever was on. In a more sombre, prestige version of this story, we'd picture people crowding round the flickering diode, nudging each other to get a look at the screen, grasping their faces in horror at discovering that JFK had been assassinated, or staring in reverence as man landed on the moon. In the more prosaic realities of rural Ireland, my father recalls only that, well into the seventies, my Great-Uncle Edward would be sure to make himself known around lunchtime on Saturdays so that he could tune into the wrestling and watch Giant Haystacks and Big Daddy beating eight shades of shite out of each other on *World of Sport*.

When my father became fascinated with genealogy, he deployed the same attention to detail; tracing the family tree as far back as any Irish person can – about 150 years, until the entire square-tentacled mass retreats back into a freckled full house of illiterate farmers, people who left no names and never troubled the government for documentation. There were some odd additions – our great-great-great-great-uncle Edward Maguire was, supposedly, the first chief of police of Chicago – but for the most part it was rustic sod-botherers, rank and file. I suppose the dream of genealogy is that you'll dig deep enough in the rough and find some shiny gem of notoriety, some improbable link to fame, fortune or foreign royalty. The best my dad could manage was his discovery that Bishop Edward Daly, a man he'd already been friends with his entire life, was very slightly related to my grandmother, a woman so close with his own mother that she had babysat the infant bishop anyway. And all *his* family had also been farmers, most definitely reared on cabbage and praties and stiff-shirted Irish republicanism. It wouldn't exactly have made a rip-roaring episode of *Who Do You Think You Are?* is what I'm saying. My father spent years at this, and basically ended up with the exact same information he would have got if he'd guessed the entire thing while very tired.

For other people this might seem like an underwhelming achievement, but for my father, who loves process above all things, the outcome was irrelevant. He loved every aspect of the search; the days in the library, the collecting of the information and its deployment in the desired datasets, the accumulation of the requisite stationery to perform each task, the architecture of the database he then used. Even the visual direction of the massive family tree itself, split among some twenty rolls of fax paper across the entire wall of his office off the garage, was a source of constant joy. But it is in that very garage office, where this family tree was displayed, that my father kept his greatest project. Not a battered wooden box of foreign spoons or a corrugated-iron hut of fatal whiskey, but fifteen to twenty small, towered cabinets containing nearly a thousand VHS tapes of films he'd recorded off the TV.

The Grand North Atlantic Home-Taped VHS Archive meant that even though we grew up in the countryside and didn't have access to Xtravision or Blockbuster, we did have a fully catalogued library of 803 films and television programmes for us to use at any time. Starved of other stimuli and tired of reading my dad's horticultural magazines, by the time I was about eight or nine I was working my way through the tape collection with the same zeal I did the bookshelves in our house, gaining a bewilderingly specific film education from an unlikely curator.

My father began the collection some time in the late eighties. The first film he taped was 0001 MY FAIR LADY, which his database helpfully informs us starred REX HARRISON and AUDREY HEPBURN. He had filed all the recordings in Lotus Approach, an early database program, which didn't have lower-case functionality, making the readouts all the more punchy and impressive.

Most usefully of all, he printed them out into a binder that we could browse at our leisure, with the entire archive listed twice; first chronologically – for the casual browser, seeking inspiration – and then alphabetically, for the man on a mission. Daddy was so excited by its capacity for information he left nothing to chance when it came to categories he opted to include within its pages. The archive declared not just the catalogue number, title and stars of each film, but also supplementary details he obviously imagined we'd find important at the time. So it is that we now know that 0001 MY FAIR LADY was recorded off BBC 2 on an E180 tape, which he bought from BOOTS. My father would also add the film's rating (U), run time (165 MIN) and, perhaps most pleasingly of all, the number of unused minutes on each tape (15). This last statistic allowed him to place multiple films on tapes of sufficient length, which was a boon for a man who might have thought he'd only be buying two or three specially designated towers of videotape storage, as opposed to the full room's worth he would eventually amass. He has, for the record, always maintained that he never intended the collection to get so big, and it just kind of grew up around him without too much forward planning. I would find this easier to believe had he not gone to the trouble of indexing all his entries with four-digit numbers, showing at least some inkling that his collection might one day number in the thousands.

Putting multiple films on tapes wasn't just a space saver, it also led to some truly memorable double bills, since a combination of curiosity and idleness would invariably mean we watched both films back to back. This had the effect of laying down incongruous associations between unconnected films, links I still can't shake. I'm so used to 0053 BUGSY MALONE and 0053A THE MUPPET MOVIE being one coherent – and excellent – viewing experience, I connect them even when I see either in any other context. A pairing of such quality was rare, since quality was not something my dad was particularly interested in, but occasionally serendipity allowed two favourites to sit together for a singularly satisfying and uninterrupted viewing experience.

More memorable still are those bewildering pairings such as 0166 PRIDE & PREJUDICE and 0166A COMMANDO, or 0569 STRICTLY BALLROOM and 0569A HIGHLANDER. These required their audience to be either especially catholic in their tastes, or in a very specific mood. Some defied classification, and needed an especially strong will to enjoy together, like the single tape that contained the second half of the Charlton Heston classic 008 BEN HUR (CONT) before the entirety of 008A CHITTY CHITTY BANG BANG. But none came close to the single, holy tape that held 0513 ROBO COP and 0513A A WOMAN'S HEART. Even the most gonzo cineaste would have been hard pressed to think of pairing Paul Verhoeven's 1987 action satire with an RTÉ concert of Irish traditional music by Mary Black, Eleanor Riordan and Maura O'Connell.

Sometimes my father's approach gestured toward the territory of high art. One example is the tape holding both 0182 POLICE ACADEMY IV and 0182A POLICE ACADEMY II, in that order, a masterpiece of mis-billing that placed two terrible films from one series back to back in the wrong order, while omitting the film that separates them in chronology. And I probably watched that tape seven or eight times.

It would be understandable for someone to read all this and presume that Daddy was a cinephile of some description, the sort of guy who lived and breathed cinema in all its forms. This would be wrong. My father enjoys films, but he's not much of a buff. He was, at best, an indifferent filmgoer and, so far as I can remember, accompanied me to the cinema only once. This was on a whole-family jaunt to see 0587 JURASSIC PARK in the Orchard Cinema housed within St Columb's Hall. This was a grand venue owned by the parish and overseen by Father Huck Balance, the self-same priest who had blessed our caravan the year before.

Here, shorn of his vestments and wearing a casual navy sweater with dog collar just visible underneath, Father Balance revealed the pleasingly venal, earthbound side of himself; he was one of those rare, one might say improbable, creatures within the Irish clergy, the parish priest with a second job – in this case, overseeing the running of the cinema and checking his punters to make sure no one was taking in sweets from outside. A Sunday morning spent declaiming from the pulpit with the stately gravitas of an aristocrat would be followed by an afternoon spent delighting at the matinee crowds, his eyes folding into dollar signs like an old-timey medicine show huckster. I think I might have seen him laughing into the till once. On this occasion in July 1993, he was practically jogging on the spot and rubbing his hands together with glee, since the crowd that day was massive.

'Ah, how are you, Joe?' he said to my dad upon our arrival, discreetly scanning each of us for the tell-tale bulge of contraband confectionery.

'Come for the dinosaurs, stay for Goldblum's best role yet,' he added, picking up a passing infant and shaking him by the ankles until some Skittles fell out.

It was nice to see this bizarro-world version of Father Huck, ordinarily quite a stern and taciturn figure. When the cinema was doing well, it seemed to give him real joy, a joy we never really saw at Mass. It didn't hurt that the parish owned the building and so he had no rent to pay on a prime location in the city centre. And even the most committed parishioner might consider the free-market implications of his having a captive audience of dedicated churchgoers. He promoted the latest releases in the parish bulletin handed out at Mass, which gave rise to some delightfully abrupt tonal shifts. On any given week, it might declare the death of a beloved member of the congregation, announce that the Vatican had just declared 1993 to be the Year of the Orphan, and end with '*He's got John Travolta's smile, Kirstie Alley's eyes and the voice of Bruce Willis, so run don't walk to the city premiere of* Look Who's Talking Too *(PG, 81 mins, NO outside consumables allowed).*'

Looking back, it seems odd that the church ran this thing on the side, not least since Father Balance genuinely appeared to have a flair for the business. He greeted the throngs of people who came to see *Jurassic Park* with an excitement that, while not being especially godly, was massively relatable. It even showcased the sort of buzzy attention to detail that seemed a bit more earnest than the mere cash grab I risk depicting here. In 1988, for example, he built up anticipation for 0352 INDIANA JONES AND THE LAST CRUSADE by playing the first two films (0477 and 0478 respectively – my father had a knack for recording these things out of order) as back-to-back features for a few weekends beforehand. While I was too young to have watched the Indiana Jones movies in the cinema, and 0458 LOOK WHO'S TALKING TOO was hardly a tentpole of my cinematic education, it's no exaggeration to say that 0587 JURASSIC PARK changed my life.

It's hard to overstate just how massively influential that film was on me, and the extent to which it became the film I judged all others against. It was not long after this that I started carrying around my little cereal box dinosaur den. It was the first film that did that to me, and the first time I realised the films I liked didn't really have the same effect on my dad. The biggest reaction he had to *Jurassic Park* was a hearty guffaw at the implication that Lex, Richard Attenborough's precocious granddaughter, would be sufficiently tech literate to operate the park's security system.

'Ha! A UNIX system?' he scoffed, out loud, in the cinema. 'Good luck!'

It wasn't that he didn't like films. Far from it – he absorbed them just as cheerily as anyone, and can be moved to tears on occasion. But for my dad, the doing of the thing was more important than the thing done; some of the things he chose to record are testament to nothing more than completist zeal. Some are clearly of personal interest: 0269 ARCHBISHOP

DALY'S INVESTITURE, which recorded our friend –
and latterly distant cousin – Bishop Daly getting his big
promotion, or 1989's 0127A COUNTRY WESTERN
MUSIC AWARDS. Neither would necessarily be present
in other people's archives but they do, at least, speak to my
father's tastes. The same can't be said for seven POLICE
ACADEMY films.

As well as a bewildering array of Northern Irish special-
interest programmes, he also included some home video he'd
shot himself, camcorder footage from holidays and christen-
ings, weddings and other family events. One notable entry is
0097A DERRY FEIS, a collection of films he'd recorded of
us singing and performing at the feis, or talent competition, at
which we competed every year, and which would surely have
tested the enthusiasm of even the most dutiful parent. The
observant reader will by now have discerned that its designation
of 0097A reveals this to be the second part of a double bill. You
will be pleased to discover this collection of indifferently performed Irish-language ballads sung by children did not follow
footage of some other social engagement, but came directly
after 0097 MAN WITH THE GOLDEN GUN, THE. Again,
you'd have to be in a very specific mood.

He added supplementary details even for those home-
shot videos. It was funny to see O'REILLY FAMILY or FR
BRIAN DARCY listed as the stars of films, interrupting an
otherwise unbroken run of Hollywood A-listers. Stirring, too,
to see the note attached to 0211 CHRISTMAS IN DERRY
1989, confirming it was FILMED ON LOCATION IN
MULLENNAN, DERRY. As a slightly tongue-in-cheek bit
of dad humour this would be quite amusing, but since I know

my father to have been entirely serious when he added these words, it's funnier still.

I'm not sure exactly when, but there was an uptick in the scale of the operation at some point in the early nineties, when my father began making improvements to the system. It had long bothered him that in order to tape a film, he'd have to be watching it, so he got a second tape recorder connected to the TV in the kitchen, which could be programmed to record there while he watched something else in the living room. Soon we had a further two machines in the garage, meaning we could, in theory, record four things at once, although I think three may have been the maximum we ever did. It should be borne in mind that we only had seven to nine channels, the four (and later five) British ones, plus three (and later four) Irish ones that existed at this time.

'If we had satellite TV,' my dad once said, 'we could be doing a lot more,' perhaps missing the point that if we did have the multiple channel options of satellite TV the need for an entire room of our house to be set aside for a videotaped content archive might be slightly reduced. Of course, having films at our fingertips via Sky Movies or Netflix or iPlayer would never have been as satisfying as going into the garage and thumbing through the binder, and finding that one thing you wanted to watch, or something you'd never heard of that would go on to be a favourite. As I got older, there was also the possibility of finding slightly more illicit thrills by looking for those films that promised intrigue, violence, or even the faint possibility of what my father considered sexiness. In theory, this was made easier by my dad's method of assigning ratings to the films, meaning surely an X would promise something to quicken the pulse. Unfortunately, my father's grasp of what constituted pornography appears to have been confused, as I discovered when I watched Warren Beatty's epic three-hour historical drama 0031 REDS, waiting for it to turn into the beach-side sex romp its X rating implied.

And Netflix can't compete with the incredible joy of finding, within those videos, that tantalising glimpse into a forgotten world which comes from the ad breaks, news segments and interstitial moments that were caught alongside the films. Around the late eighties and early nineties, Northern Irish television was broadly indistinguishable from its Soviet counterpart, and each evening's programming was 'presented' by an announcer, or more commonly a pair of announcers, who sat on couches and addressed the viewer with details of the next programme. There are few experiences headier than watching UTV's Julian Simmons gamely introducing 0421A DIE HARD after having just recapped *Coronation Street* in his ear-melting Belfast twang.

There's something bracing about the nostalgia produced by old news segments and ads, something ephemeral and throw-away, caught and held in suspension. As if pulling the camera back from whatever movie we were hoping to watch and training it on our own unwashed world. The place we were trying to escape, full of mullets and double denim and burning cars, punctured only by the desultory glamour of the glitzier advertisements of the time – camels pouring foaming pints of bright yellow Harp lager, beaming ladies in tight jeans driving Renault Clios, a puzzling number of people all declaring their desire for Chicken Tonight.

Back then, adverts were often just place cards displayed for thirty seconds with an excitable voice overlaid. 'Discover Fashion,' it might say, breathily, as an ethereal chorus repeated 'fashion ... fashion ... fashion' into the background, like a group of sexy, couture-mad Northern Irish angels retreating backwards into a mist of giant hair and shoulder pads. This was only ever very slightly undercut by the legend underneath declaring said outlet store had now re-opened, following a closure due to bomb damage. I have never been to the Spinning Wheel pub in Castlertownroche, Co. Cork, nor the town itself, but I will never forget that it was open for business and spent no small part of its marketing budget on letting me and everyone else in Ireland know all about it.

At certain points, looking through this binder now as a grown man, there comes a melancholy sense of fossilised effort, something heart-breaking about the project. I get a faint pluck at the eyelid when I imagine Daddy alone in our garage, filling out the run time (140mins), tape make (SCOTCH) and classification (U) of desultory 1987 TV movie 0262 ASSAULT AND MATRIMONY. Not least since he evidently forgot he had this classic nailed down and recorded it again when it was repeated as 0275 ASSAULT & MATRIMONY. It was sometimes quite evident he wasn't sure what he was recording and was either doing it for our benefit or just to add another film to the stock. Nowhere is this clearer than my favourite bit of writing in the entire collection, where he lists the John Hughes romantic comedy *She's Having a Baby*, with masterful stuffiness, as 0418 SHE IS HAVING A BABY.

It's easier to make fun of it as a hare-brained way of dodging video rental fees, or the massive, nerdy compulsion of someone who loved AV technology and databases. I see within it a kernel of my own preferred way of organising grief; pushing unknowables out of my mind by cramming in enough verifiable data that I'm kept occupied. Maybe the archive was my dad's way of making sense out of chaos, to create a system, however arbitrary, that could approximate all the ordered specificity our world must have lacked at that time.

I spent a large part of my childhood and adolescence wondering if my father and I had much in common at all. And I think our love of archiving is the biggest thing, a bulwark against the terror of losing. Everything in its one right, good and true place, safe from harm.

By the time I was in my early teens, my siblings and I had taken the work of the archive over from my dad, who didn't feel the need to tape everything any more. It was up to us to record those things we needed to be saved. I'd like to be able to tell you that the last entry I compiled was 0644 DEER HUNTER, a taut, moving classic that deals with loss, death and fragile masculinity. But it was an unmemorable 1983 drama, 0645A LORDS OF DISCIPLINE, THE, and it wasn't even filmed properly. The footage stutters before we're catapulted to the film's end, with forty minutes unaccounted for. After the credits, we're greeted by UTV's continuity announcers, Mike and Linda, once more looking out to us from their beige couches.

There they sit, telling us what else they have planned for broadcast tonight and for the rest of the weekend, as if we are guests in their oddly flat, uncomfortable home, which appears to be nothing more than two front-facing couches, a clock and an endless vault of TV programmes they've taken it upon themselves to choose for our nightly entertainment. You needn't worry about us, though, Mike and Linda. We have a garage, a binder and the whole world in front of us.

12

Notable
Explosions, 1988–2005

After Daddy had his leg cut off, I didn't see him laugh again
until the pope died. Not that the expiry of His Holiness was,
in and of itself, hilarious. It was just that Robert Dalton told him
that Reservoir Meats, the meat-packing plant about a mile from
our house, ended up briefly closing because of it, which reduced
Daddy to tears of ungovernable laughter, while the bandages were
still wet in his hospital bed. Robert – the kindly farmer who was
good enough to take me out for a day on his tractor when I was
six – was a very dear friend of my father. As well as farming, he
had a job as the local meat inspector, surveying the premises of
slaughterhouses, packing plants and abattoirs, making sure they
stood up to government code, which placed him in that rare
bracket of health and safety officers who might mark down your
workplace if it had insufficient sharp objects and too few vats of
animal blood. Most of his time was taken up, I gather, scrutinising

the cleanliness and work practices of large blood-stained buildings in Derry and the north-west, making sure people weren't licking the carcasses or incorrectly storing barrels filled with hooves.

Reservoir Meats was something of a community success. Many Northern Ireland businesses don't have mixed workforces of Catholics and Protestants, even today. Sometimes this is a function of geography, but it's also a legacy of sectarian hiring practices that worked as a barrier for Catholics. For decades it was, for example, prohibitively difficult for a Catholic to work in Belfast's shipyards or gain entrance to trades through apprenticeships, as these were often closed to papists. Reservoir Meats was, by contrast, an egalitarian employer, one in which working-class Catholics and Protestants sat side by side all day, chopping up animal cadavers with giant cleavers, passing their time in an atmosphere that bordered on bonhomie.

This was despite, or perhaps because of, a culture of bristlingly offensive discourse between groups. Where other workforces might slag off each other's chosen football team or questionable fashion choices, here the jokes threw off references to punishment beatings, political murders and tit-for-tat killings amid a demographic of people who more than likely had direct experience of one or more in their own immediate families. Both of my brothers would come home from their shifts, white-faced and staring, having spent eight hours squeezed between huge men with hands like shovels, their own willowy, teenaged forms almost comically tiny and mute compared to their beefy neighbours with scarred knuckles and paramilitary tattoos, tearing meat apart as they traded withering barbs.

'Is your cousin still missing, Gerry?' one might say to his opposite, provoking laughter from the whole room and from

Gerry himself, suggesting that the abduction and murder of a family member was not just an allowable subject for humour, but one even its target had to agree was, at the end of the day, hilarious. All such jibes were taken in good humour, or rather something like the blithe nihilism that becomes general in any place where people have lived through thirty years of violent conflict and now dismantle animal corpses for a living. These were men who might, at one time, have been at war with each other. Now they sat together pulling raw beef from leg joints and shoulder sockets all day, and would drink, bet and play darts with each other afterwards. This was some strange, blood-splattered version of peace in our time, so what harm was there in throwing off a joke about your disappeared cousin?

In comparison, ridiculing the pope's death should have been small potatoes. Given John Paul II's declining health over that year, it was entirely predictable. The Protestant workers' most waggish contingent had already been singing mock Latin when news had come in that Il Papa was too weak to give Easter Mass. By the time he died, and they showed up wearing black arm-bands, Robert told us it was received with relative equanimity by the other side, except for one particular group: the plant's thirty Polish workers, who, quite aside from being ardent Catholics, were particularly invested in the first-ever Polish pope. It appears likely that the everyday jibes had passed them by, since they so often centred on local politics and personal histories and were delivered in that machine-gun Derry accent that's only variably comprehensible to people from Northern Ireland, let alone the Baltic states. During the minute's silence that was held, it was harder for the Poles to ignore their workmates' jeering shouts of 'fuck the pope' and 'dirty Polish bastard'. Quite rightly horrified, the Poles went on strike, grinding the plant to a halt for days, interrupting the meat supply to the region and putting the entire business in jeopardy.

It was this story, delivered in Robert's signature south Derry monotone, that had my dad in literal and figurative stitches in the amputation ward. Despite being a Catholic who loved and admired Pope John Paul II, who had even sent two of his daughters to sing for the man, my dad found the whole thing unaccountably hilarious for exactly the same reason I did: so many horrific, depressing and awful things have happened in Northern Ireland in his lifetime that whatever joy can be taken from incidents in which no one was physically harmed will be seized with both hands.

Contradictions like this – my extremely Catholic father laughing his head off in a hospital bed at news of Protestant slaughtermen mocking the pope's death – are hard to explain to people who aren't from Northern Ireland. There's a gallows humour that freaks them out, and they don't know how they should react. Sometimes I think the only good thing about being from Northern Ireland is that, unlike people from everywhere else, I'm not inherently scared of Northern Irish people. We are the coeliac vegans of the UK and Ireland; whatever you offer, we might take offence. Part of it is due to people's perception of us as either humourless, recreationally offended victims, or violent psychopaths incapable of getting along with each other.

Robert, while a dear friend of my father's, was also a committed loyalist who belonged to the Apprentice Boys of Derry, a Protestant fraternal organisation similar to the Orange Order. They march through Derry every year to commemorate the 1689 siege in which the Protestant inhabitants of the city's walled section successfully repelled the Catholic forces of King James, keeping it Protestant in the process. The Apprentice Boys have traditionally been regarded with resentment and hatred by the city's Catholic majority, since they celebrate the imposition of centuries of religious suppression. The ideals of Protestant supremacy espoused by such orders were effectively the law in Northern Ireland well into my father's lifetime, barring Catholics from prominent positions and trades, and withholding civil and political rights. Housing provision for Catholics was infamously appalling, and since only property owners could vote in local elections, the entire Catholic population of Derry was effectively disenfranchised until the late sixties.

My father didn't have an inalienable right to vote until he was very nearly thirty, while my mother's parents, who never owned a house in their entire lives, were in their late fifties by the time they cast their first local ballot. The Apprentice Boys' own marches, once highly contentious in Derry, have become less so of late, although there's really little to be said in defence of an organisation that still doesn't admit Catholics and bars its members from attending Catholic services or events. Despite all this, my father refused to judge Robert, or anyone else, based on their membership of this or that organisation, in a belief that life was too short to start pulling at these threads, since such things were as much grounded in circumstance, parentage and tradition as hard-felt convictions one way or the other. For me, and people of my generation, this stance was simultaneously weirdly admirable and maddeningly complacent. For my father it was nothing more complicated than knowing a person by their deeds rather than their political stripe.

*

The Derry Journal,
Tuesday 30 August 1988

WEEKEND OF CHAOS

Derry was returning to near normality yesterday after one of the worst weekends of violence in recent years. During the widespread disturbances a RUC man was injured, a customs post was destroyed, seven houses were badly damaged and 21 stained glass windows were destroyed in St Columb's Cathedral by an IRA bomb, and Derry City centre was thrown into chaos by a series of bomb scares and hijackings ... on Friday night a masked man in a black Mazda car drove into a filling station on the Northern side of the border at Molenan Road and fired four to five shots into the air shouting bomb warnings at two border customs posts before driving back into Donegal.

About an hour later a loud explosion was heard in the Letterkenny Road area. The area was sealed off on both sides of the border by RUC and Garda personnel and on Saturday morning it was discovered that the unmanned British customs post at Molenan had been destroyed.

The IRA claimed responsibility for both explosions.

When the IRA detonated a bomb at the top of our road on 27 August 1988, it wasn't particularly big news. Not to me, certainly, since I was just shy of my third birthday, but neither to the watching world. The above snippet from our local paper came out four days later, and limited the mention of the 'Molenan Road' explosion – *our* explosion – to about fifty words, sandwiched in between other, more notable incidents from 'one of the worst weekends of violence in recent years'. As someone who spent so much of his life struggling for the praise, adulation and attention I deserved, I find it typical that even the IRA bomb that damaged my house was considered insignificant in comparison to other more impressive bombs with which it had to share its moment. I hear you, plucky little bomb. It's also typical that the only thing my dad deemed worthy of comment when I dug up this article was the fact they misspelled the name of our street, Mullennan Road.

The explosion took apart the customs post which was, in reality, little more than a prefabricated hut that you could have talked into coming down. Maybe that's what the 'shouted bomb warnings' were an actual attempt at achieving. Since the building had the structural density of a pack of Super Noodles, the explosion ejected quite a spectacular amount of debris, and bits of badly made building flew into our field. These included, most pleasingly of all, a wall that had a lavatory sink still attached. We were home at the time, although our three eldest were holidaying in Wicklow with Mammy's friend Patricia. The army cordoned off the area and, fearing that unexploded ordnance might still be nearby, evacuated our house. We spent the next few days at my grandfather's in Fermanagh, expanding the population of his small council house – two elderly people – to eleven and a half, with the addition of seven children under ten, plus Daddy, and Mammy, who was just recently recovering from cancer treatment and also seven months pregnant with Conall.

This was all deemed so uninteresting that I wasn't even told about it until my dad mentioned it well into my twenties, in the sort of offhand way you might tell someone who was sure they'd never ridden a donkey that they had, in fact, ridden a donkey, but when they were too young to remember it. Even Shane was unimpressed when Mammy rang Patricia to tell her about it, to the extent that he tried to one-up her news by telling her Patricia added fresh bananas to the Weetabix every morning, a worldly affectation that was quite exotic to us; certainly more so than some bomb or other going off.

We were, of course, more worldly than we realised, despite my parents' best efforts to shield us. A good Catholic was to be in this world but not of it. For some that meant totally swearing off all temptations of the modern world, but for us it meant little more than restricted access to cartoons. My dad hadn't accounted for me getting up two or three hours before him each morning to gorge on them. For years, I would wake up in the small hours and assemble a ramshackle fort by the TV in the kitchen. This was achieved by the time-honoured route of sticking two chairs front to front and stretching a duvet over both in such a way that I was covered but could still view the children's programming that began around 6 a.m. This was the only way of getting TV into my system each morning, since Daddy's loyalty was to the homespun, newsy charm of BBC Radio Foyle. Mornings in our house began with a roar from my father to get up and then the radio in the kitchen filtering through the house at factory-floor volume. This dispensed a steady drone of traffic reports from hilly back roads, cheerless pronouncements by local politicians and the dispiritingly regular death notices that proliferated through my childhood. Here, each freshly ended life, along with the killing's location – 'outside his home', 'while on holiday', 'on the Lisburn Road' – would be recited without emotion. It's odd to look back and consider that this litany of death was considered somehow more age-appropriate and wholesome than cartoons in which toys beat each other up.

Where we were raised, in the countryside, Protestants and Catholics got along, and in our spare time we participated regularly in ecumenical activities: school trips and deliberately mixed social events. Our whole family attended cross-community summer camps in Corrymeela, a community hub in Ballycastle where mixed religious services were held and people gathered in big tents for events and talks that went heavy with words like 'reconciliation' and 'dialogue'. Here you might hear reformed paramilitaries sharing their stories, preaching forgiveness and embracing each other on stage as if they were competing city contractors who'd put aside their differences to launch a shopping centre rather than men who'd spent decades placing increasingly large explosive devices near each other's heads. It was moving, and formative in a way that I couldn't then comprehend. Not just the big-ticket moments of on-stage redemption, but simpler things like playing football or doing arts and crafts courses with Alistairs and Margarets and Gregorys who might otherwise have grown up twenty

202

minutes from our house without ever talking to a Séamas or a Caoimhe.

Even now, these sound like asinine and self-congratulatory platitudes. It seems bland and obvious to say, 'Wow, we're all the same when you think about it.' It's the sort of hackneyed, government-issue reconciliation twaddle that would be on the nose if it were painted on the side of a youth centre. But it's also true. These mundane experiences, and the quiet revelations we gained from them, were rare at the time. They for ever affirmed the falseness of those arbitrary separations that were said to exist between our communities. They emphasised the banal uniformity of our upbringings and the contrivance of those differences held up even by sober and responsible referees as something in-bred, deeply held and fiercely owned. Four days later I'd be back in school, where I might well have been the only seven-year-old in my class who had Protestant friends.

Derry city itself, where we all went to school, was a bit less kumbaya about 'the other side'. Direct, unalloyed sectarianism was pretty much everywhere. A breezily casual hatred for the British in particular, and Protestantism in general, was like a constant white noise that accompanied daily life. Bartie Harkin and Con Huckstable were both given notes from their parents stating that they wished their child be withdrawn from PE if rugby or cricket were to be played. (Football, though every bit as British, was excepted from this because it was a sport that Catholics liked.) Euclid Duddy was so republican his family banned his sisters from listening to the Spice Girls after Geri wore the Union Jack dress. I once attended a birthday party at his house, and his dad, Ron, took each of us aside at different points and gave us an increasingly sozzled blow-by-blow account of the events of Bloody Sunday.

Ron Duddy was the sort of man who got up at dawn so he could hate the Brits that bit longer each day. He told me they killed Kennedy to stop an Irish Catholic having his day in the sun, and banned the family from using any laundry service in the Bogside because he'd heard the washing machines were fitted with chemical analysers that would detect explosives on your clothes and arrest you on the spot. It was left to you – a child attending his son's ninth birthday party – to speculate as to how much explosive residue his clothes may have contained. He had steeped his son in such a rich stew of paranoid republicanism that Euclid would often boast that he'd never met a Protestant. These were the extremes, but there was everywhere the sort of quotidian anti-British sentiment that hung around like fog, or the acrid smoke of rifles emptied into defenceless teenagers.

We poked fun at people like Ron, but at a young age he had watched neighbourhood children, some of whom were family and close friends, killed by soldiers who never faced any consequences for their actions, and who were still present on his streets decades later. Any modern analysis would say Ron and large portions of the city were going through a mass bout of post-traumatic stress disorder. Since this was years before PTSD was effectively treated, and decades before it became a household word, many Northern Irish people remained untouched by counselling or medication. It was easier to throw stones at police or redirect your negative energy at a formless, shapeless approximation of Britain. Even to me, who had been sheltered from so much, it was patently obvious that we were the good guys and the British were the evil empire, a contention backed up by pretty much all Irish, British and American films and television programmes we watched; in fact, by any content that wasn't made specifically by Northern Irish unionists. That said, some of the hatred was so confused as to be hilarious. The Sex Pistols' 'God Save the Queen' was once booed in the Gweedore pub, presumably because people had heard the first four words of the song and misinterpreted it as a sincere paean to Elizabeth II.

For years, Reebok Classics that were extremely sought after everywhere else in the UK were sold in Derry at a loss, since each pair came with a small, but unmistakable, Union flag just below the tongue. To sneaker aficionados elsewhere, this was a mark of quality, but to Derry folk they might as well have been pre-soiled with dogshit.

My parents did an incredible job of guiding us away from hatred and horror, but there were certain things from which they couldn't protect us, or to which they had simply become so inured it would never have occurred to them to do so. They had both experienced discrimination as very visible Catholics, but never became bitter or fearful. I could see the tension in my father when we were barked at by soldiers, had to go through checkpoints, or when we might pass an 'incident' wreathed by police tape and held down by armoured cars. And these things were pretty common. Of all my memories of my mother, the only one with a feeling attached is that of the bomb scare on that bus near Moore Walk – not just the look on my mother's face, but the squeeze of her fist around mine, her clammy hand and hurried breath. I remember that she never said the words 'bomb scare' but I heard them from the other passengers, who said them not with terror but the sort of low-grade annoyance you get when a self-service checkout says 'unexpected item' and you have to go through the indignity of summoning a distant Sainsbury's checkout assistant as if asking the teacher if you can go to the toilet.

Living under a cloud of bomb threats and extrajudicial murder doesn't necessarily leave you in a state of constant fear. What can break your spirit is the deadening trudge of small humiliations and the steady expectation of petty inconvenience. It's life being interrupted by a hundred things outside your control. These were things that parents – our parents – tried to hurry past without mentioning to us. Subjects were changed and plans for the day amended. Everyone in my class had a story of their mum rapidly abandoning some expedition and being really nice all of a sudden. Yes, they'd say, we were supposed to be going to the swimming baths. Yes, we're going a different way now. Yes, we can stop for a treat on the way. Certainly, these 'incidents' increased immeasurably the prospect of us getting ice cream or a Lucky Bag for no reason. For those sugary treats and cheap plastic toys, we all had the Provisional IRA to thank.

There were other things about that time which I don't think my parents could have known were wrinkling my little brain, and certainly weren't countered with restorative balms of junk food or Lucky Bags. The news my father listened to each morning, with its daily metronome of murder announcements, terror attacks and notable explosions, was all the more horrifying for the blankness with which they were issued. Its delineations of Northern Ireland's communities, too, were less black and white than those of Ron Duddy, but not by much. They still reflected and endorsed the same separation, the cataloguing of people by tribe. Any death reported was tagged with the victim's religious affiliation, in a manner that was doubtless ethnographically useful but also diminutive and absurd.

'*Samuel Marshall, Catholic*', '*James and Ellen Sefton, both Protestant*'.

Again, it's hard to think of another way they could have done it, since this was a time when tit-for-tat killings were commonplace and entirely innocent people all over Northern Ireland were being murdered by paramilitaries simply because an opposing faction had murdered one of 'their' side the day before. These people were not targeted for their involvement in politics or activism, but merely to spread terror through the enemy: that any of 'you' could be got, no matter your actual beliefs or political activity. This was the motive for hundreds of murders, meaning it was, in a real sense, relevant that things be recorded in this manner, while simultaneously being oddly impersonal and dehumanising when they were. Leaving aside the sense it gave of some great big score card in the sky, it reduced the sole piece of identifying information to the religion foisted upon the victims by their parents, which, odds were, meant little to them other than the fact it was reason enough to be killed by the roaming death cults that blighted Northern Ireland at the time. If you'd never been to church in your life and were murdered in your home, your birth religion would be mentioned before your name in the headlines, especially if you had the indignity to be killed as part of a group.

'*4 Catholics Shot Dead on the Ormeau Road*' or '*The RUC are appealing for information, regarding the murders of 3 Protestant men near the Glenshane Pass this morning'.*

You could have spent your life curing polio or inventing the Harrier jet, but as long as you were a non-famous Northern Irish person murdered by paramilitaries, your childhood attendance of a Church of Ireland school was paramount. Only in other cases – weird cases, involving non-Northern Irish casualties – would something like normal reportage prevail. When the IRA killed two Australian lawyers in the Netherlands, in the mistaken belief that they were off-duty British soldiers, it made no sense to report those people's religions; unlike me and my family, they hadn't been stupid enough to be born in Northern Ireland and thus had not, at birth, been signed up for the whole bizarre charade.

Robert was a good friend to us, even those of us who weren't gifted young farmers. When my mother died, he came to the funeral even though the rules of his organisation expressly forbade attendance at any Catholic event. This sounds like a commonplace act of decency, but my father was immeasurably touched by it, and touched too by the work friends and neighbours of that persuasion who, though refusing to enter the church itself, stood vigil outside the building for the duration and re-joined the cortège thereafter. Their friendship naturally extended to Robert's being at my father's bedside in hospital, just in time to tell him about the goings-on in Reservoir Meats.

My father's diabetes should have been spotted earlier, since his diet had been pretty bad for a while. Never particularly keen to begin with, he'd started swearing off vegetables entirely, declaring that he'd only ever eaten them so that we would.

To this day he can't say the word broccoli without mock retching. Brussels sprouts he calls 'wee green round bastards'. Throughout my childhood, he insisted on a forensic examination of Christmas puddings every year, eating a different one each Sunday in the weeks and months running up to the big day, recording his findings and debating their qualities with us, so that through this exacting process we could crown a winner. We eventually noticed that this tournament was starting earlier and earlier each year, with preliminary rounds beginning in September and even August. By the time of my brother Shane's wedding, he'd taken to keeping a stash of fizzy drinks in his bedroom, hidden in a wardrobe as if they were heroin or plastic explosives. He had, paradoxically, lost a lot of weight, and his circulation had clearly deteriorated. At the ceremony I noticed a cut on his hand from fixing a mower at home. By the time Shane and Becky had returned from honeymoon several weeks later it hadn't healed.

Things progressed from there. I was at university in Dublin when I heard a cut on his foot had become severely infected and the toe would need to be removed, then several toes, then the whole foot and then further and further up. The entire saga was obviously a huge shock to my dad, who had not been aware of the seriousness of his condition, but, losing time to the spread of infection, it was he who said he was prepared to get ahead of the problem by having the surgeons cut just below his right knee. There would be a long hard road from there on out, with the physical and emotional strains of recovery, rehab and adaptation to his prosthesis, but he attacked it with the same unshowy stoicism with which he'd tackled everything else, barring broccoli, the death of Joe Dolan or the four out of ten

I once gave a Tesco Finest Melt-in-the-Middle Chocolate and Salted Caramel Christmas Pudding for Six.

In the immediate aftermath of the surgery he was bullish and confident, although a lot of that might have been the effects of shock and/or morphine. There was also the sense of what could have gone wrong, since the amputation had, after all, averted possible death. When I came home to see him I was a complete wreck, and quizzed my brother Shane through nervy tears.

'How is he?'

'He's grand,' breezed Shane, before adding with a beam, 'He wants the other leg off!'

This was the first time I had laughed since hearing the news, but it took Robert to get the first laugh out of Daddy. For the most part, people were extremely nervous around him, scared of how serious the problem had been, and perhaps of the physical horror of amputation. My dad had hated pity as a widower and now hated it as an amputee, and so insisted on thrusting his stump out of the sheets and into full view of any person who walked in with their sheepish mouth and trembling hands. Once you'd been through it, it was fun to watch others be subjected to the same. This was his own version of slaughterhouse wit, the gallows humour that kept the horror at bay.

It was immediately apparent just how many phrases and aphorisms revolve around feet, as when my sister Maeve made reference to the staff nurse keeping Daddy 'on his toes' and making sure he 'toed the line', two phrases I can't imagine her using in any other circumstance. The delightful Sister Francistine, the nun who was the principal of our primary school, came to counsel my father and ended her visit by agreeing it was no use being negative. 'You just have to take each day as it comes,' she said, 'and put your best … face … forward.' We said nothing. 'Um,' she added so quietly it was hard not to laugh in her face, 'is that the phrase?' Whether it was before, it certainly was after, and has been a favourite in our family ever since.

My dad's resilience was remarkable, and within a few weeks of coming home from hospital he had mastered his prosthesis to the point where he could ride a bike fairly easily. This was particularly surprising to us, since he hadn't been seen on a bike for maybe upwards of a decade and hasn't been seen on one since. When he returned to work, he didn't make a big fuss about what had happened, and didn't bother telling his more casual acquaintances, who often had no idea about the prosthesis and presumed he just had a slight limp. This led to complications once, when he slipped and fell on an office visit to Belfast. It was, luckily, a minor fall, more embarrassing than anything else, although it momentarily dislodged his prosthetic leg. As he winced on the floor, pride dented but physically unharmed, a colleague took him by the hand and looked in horror at the unwelcome right angle that had formed in my father's trouser leg. 'Jesus!' he said, thinking my father hadn't yet noticed his shinbone snapping in two. 'It's a bad fall, Joe.' You might not find that story funny, but when I tell it to Northern Irish people, it kills.

The aftercare my father received from the hospital included offers of meetings, rehab activity programmes and support groups for people dealing with amputations, all of which he declined. I'd say it was because he wanted to move on, or because he didn't want to be defined by his disability, but it's more likely he simply couldn't be arsed. He had spent so much time in hospital that he had no interest in going back for non-essential purposes, let alone hanging out with loads of new people into the bargain. In the first few weeks after the amputation, I noted the stack of unread pamphlets he'd been sent, advertising local get-togethers and sporting events for the benefit and interest of Northern Irish amputees. We laughed bleakly, unforgivably, as we saw that the legacy of the Troubles had monopolised even these, and that 90 per cent of the people featured in their articles were people who'd been injured in sectarian fighting, not those who stashed Fanta and organised annual world cups of rich, sweet desserts.

'I could go with you,' I said, 'and tell them you lost the leg when the customs hut was destroyed. Taken out by a flying sink, maybe. That way you won't lose *feet* – I mean *face*. Is that the phrase?' We drove to the hospital, finding comfort in the laughter of the slaughterhouse, and through tears he told me just how awful I was.

13

Dead and Dying Cows

A few years before we were married, my wife and I took a city break to Bilbao, which did not go to plan. We hadn't been on holiday for a long time and booked the cheap deal on a whim about a month before we were to travel. I don't know what our plan actually was, but by the time the trip came around we hadn't received the windfall we'd clearly been expecting to fund it, and subsequently had to slum it the entire time, with no cash beyond what we had to spend on transport and accommodation. My wife, a vegetarian, found there was almost nothing she could eat in any of the places we visited, and on more than one occasion her requests for a fully vegetarian salad were met with grilled chicken served with anchovy sauce. The rain was so bad that the only shoes I had with me became waterlogged within a few hours of our arrival and were noticeably smelly by the second day of an unjustifiably lengthy four-day visit. My feet swelled up, and more than once I'm sure other tourists moved away from me. One French gentleman pointed at my limp and sodden shoe and said, 'Ze trench foot, yes?'

For three more days I took tired, smelly steps around a city that might charitably be said to contain two good days' worth of tourism, with a First World War foot disease, under a wet mesh of rain that poured, ceaselessly, from a sky the colour of a switched-off telly. The only great memory that survives is of the Guggenheim, which we liked so much we visited three times. I was struck by Louise Bourgeois's *Maman*, the thirty-foot sculpture of a spider that towers over its rear entrance.

Before I learned to package all the stuff I knew into the kind of A+ anecdotes for which I'm so rightly celebrated, I settled for simply following people around while I reeled off random facts: species of dinosaurs, collective nouns for animals, rare types of clouds, particularly snazzy prime numbers. And spiders. I knew loads about spiders. So when I read in the brochure that Bourgeois intended this big bronze monster, jealously guarding its abdominal clutch of marble-hewn eggs, as a tribute to mothers and motherhood, I knew this was bollocks. Spiders are terrible mothers. No maternal instinct at all. Spider mams just fuck off, and it's left to the dad to collect, guard and then lick the eggs into shape, cowering on whatever godforsaken leaf she's left him on until, finally, they burst in their hundreds, sending a spindly mass of spiderlings crawling all over his pliant, furry body. A process I refuse to believe even a spider wouldn't find extremely upsetting.

I found myself saying all of this to my future wife like a crazy person. I had no idea where it was coming from. My eyes buzzed and my throat felt hot. I broke down, possessed with a baffling sense of indignation that spider mams had been let off the hook by the whims of this deluded sculptor. The rage came fully formed from many years of telling people these specific spider-mam facts.

Shortly afterwards I was seized by a deep embarrassment for my childhood self. I couldn't help imagining how I must have sucked the air out of the room when I said all this stuff about spider mams to adults: a motherless fact-merchant braying about maternal abandonment, utterly oblivious to how clearly it reflected my own grief and sadness and anger. In that moment, I knew two things: firstly, that there were still things I'd not emotionally grappled with in twenty years; and secondly, that I was right about spiders, and Louise Bourgeois should have looked it up.

This was not my first breakdown. I first realised I was depressed one morning in 1996, as an old lady was telling me IRA bombers just weren't what they used to be. Fay Poultice was probably only sixty or so, but seemed ancient to my ten-year-old self. I often sat beside her on the bus, since my siblings and I rarely sat together on the way to school. It seems odd now, but it could be we were getting our recommended daily allowance of each other at home and relished the opportunity to sit in the company of others, even if they spent the entire journey wearing the ears off us with absurd pronouncements, as Fay did. Fay insisted the concept of lunch was a new invention that hadn't existed when she was a child and was likely concocted to make money for people who made sandwiches, which she detested on account of them being 'common'. She was the first person I'd ever heard speculate about chemtrails, the theory that the cloudy emissions seen trailing aeroplanes are not emissions at all, but a cocktail of nefarious chemicals the government showers on the populace for a variety of effects. American conspiracy theorists posit that these chemicals make us more obedient and compliant. Fay thought their purpose was merely to stain clothes just after you'd hung them out, forcing the plain people of Ireland to buy more washing powder. As we watched the Derry countryside hurtle past our window, Fay would declaim on all things under the sun, while passing me Fox's Glacier Mints. These she took from a small sewing tin she carried just for sweets, palming them off to me with one pinch of her baggy hand, plopping them into my paw with fingers so spindly her knuckles looked like knots tied in an empty glove. Fay spoke often of her husband, a man so frugal it bordered on the folkloric. He was so abstemious, she said, that he'd switch the gas off while he turned his bacon, would skin a louse for a ha'penny, and if ever he found a plaster he'd cut himself. I never met Mr Poultice, but his wife's slanders were so regular and so scabrous that I had barely flinched, aged seven, when she told me 'that cunt would peel an orange in his pocket'.

I usually chatted along amiably with Fay, delighted to hear the insights of someone who addressed me as an adult, but on that particular morning I hadn't slept properly in weeks. Too withdrawn to contribute, I rubbed the bags under my eyes as she filled the silence with another of her favourite topics: the IRA bombings that had been prevalent in England since the end of the ceasefire earlier that year. Fay spoke about bombings as if they were weather events. If she reflected on a 'mild' or a 'bad' weekend, she meant in terms of the explosive content of the news and would expound at length on any incidents I might have missed. Her interest struck me, even at the time, as oddly detached. I

216

never heard her utter a single word in favour of republicanism as an ideal. It was more as though she was giving me the football scores. She recounted each casualty, and the strategies by which they were wrought, with the same dour affect she used when talking about a new post office in Moville, or the names and numbers of pills she had to take for the good of her legs.

'Bus bomb in Aldwych, killed the young lad carrying it.'

'Five pound of Semtex on the Charing Cross Road. Left in a phone box. Controlled explosion.'

Fay loved a controlled explosion. Everyone loved controlled explosions, since they were always the best footage on the news. Amid the sad faces and drizzly rain of Northern Irish life, there was something futuristically charming about Wheelbarrow, the little robot they sent in to trigger them. Wheelbarrow looked like a tiny crane mounted on tank tracks, and the combination of its ungainly form and jerky remote-control movements gave it a tragicomic quality every time it rolled over to a parked car or wheelie bin, obliviously trundling toward certain death.

Local bombings were less frequent now, so when her itinerary of away matches was over she filled more silence describing how easy it would be to bomb each place we passed. Fay saw the world as a wide-open field of knolls, crannies, bottlenecks and pinch points, all of which a bomber – a smarter class of bomber, I surmised – might exploit. 'One could go off by the pillar box there, another two in a van at the other end – total carnage.' 'If you blew up a flatbed there, all the traffic would be blocked up and it'd be like shooting fish in a barrel after that.' There was an air of disappointment in the way she described these hypothetical insurgencies, as if she'd do a better job, given the chance. Luckily for all concerned, she lacked any such inclination.

Besides, her husband had sold the car that could have helped her get to and from her detonations, on the grounds it wasn't cost-effective with the bus only a mile down the road.

Interactions of this kind were fairly standard. The bus driver, Fintan, was a paunchy man from the west of Ireland who would have been an unlikely candidate for the job, even if he hadn't looked uncannily like Hitler, which, in fact, he did. He appeared to despise his work and had a hatred of children matched only by a fondness for swearing and an alarming indifference to road safety. Fintan screamed at traffic lights and growled at babies, and behaved as if driving the bus was ruining other, more important plans he'd scheduled for that morning. It wasn't even a dedicated school bus. Fintan's was the main Bus Éireann coach from Ballybofey to Derry, which crossed the border in front of our house twice a day in each direction, and usually ten minutes either side of its scheduled time. More than once it didn't stop at all, galloping cheerfully past us as if the handful of schoolchildren waving their arms in the pouring rain were a charming roadside attraction best admired at high speed.

And high speed was the order of the day. If my dad drove as if he had an injured child in the back of his vehicle, Fintan drove as if he was the fella who'd run them over. If he did pick you up, you had roughly four seconds to ascend the stairs, receive your growl and proffer your bus pass or change. You'd barely have time to think that man really does look like Hitler before the door clanged shut like a bear trap and the bus pummelled onward. More than once his accelerative zeal prompted a clatter of tiny limbs, as infants who failed to take their seats were scattered like limp little skittles along the coach's central aisle.

*

218

I was usually delighted to hear the insights of people who addressed me like an adult, to learn about the running feuds Fay had with her hairdresser and offer what consolation I could when she told me Mr Poultice had spent another November week refusing to stick the heating on. My lack of interest in joining in as Fay issued her regular commentary on bombs and bombing was a grave sign that I was no longer capable of enjoying anything.

Some time in February 1996, I stopped sleeping. Each evening, a chill would settle in my stomach after I came in from school, suspending me in a fog of anxiety I couldn't shake. A sad, stringy tension seized me as bedtime approached, and my mind swarmed with dread. I couldn't place what was wrong, only that this formless feeling was pervasive, and I'd spend every evening in fear of the sleeplessness ahead.

I was ten. Insomnia had never been a problem. I was that child who could sleep on a chicken's lip. Hot cars, busy ferries, sun-blasted poolside lounging chairs – I never needed more than a few minutes before I was completely unconscious. Sleep was an old friend who'd never given me any trouble but now bore me some unaccountable grudge. It was like forgetting how to blink, or breathe.

Each night in bed, my brain edged toward drowsiness and I circled my fatigue with paranoid attention, intent on making its dull spark catch fire. This only prolonged the agony until I was wider awake than before, and the whole cycle would repeat until some meagre, restless half-sleep was achieved. At first, the horror was confined to nights, the evenings, but soon the knowledge of what was coming would creep into afternoons, until I was in a constant state of tired dread. A heaviness swirled once my head hit the pillow, relenting only when I finally collapsed with exhaustion around 5 a.m. I awoke at seven to a fear of having to get through yet another day and night.

Weeks turned into months. Fatigue made me sloppy and confused in school. I grew more sullen and withdrawn, staring vacantly in class, picking at my food at mealtimes. I lost weight, and brown-beige bags grew under my eyes like coffee stains. I don't remember saying anything about any of this to my family. It felt as though what was happening was on the edge of speech, or something I would be ashamed to say out loud. I don't think anyone noticed anything. There were nine of us living at home at this stage, each of us as self-absorbed as the next, so a failure to spot one sibling acting a bit more mopey than usual was probably understandable.

Whether brought on by stress, lack of sleep or the ravages upon my diet, I eventually developed severe abdominal pains and had to be brought to the doctor. Our GP was Phillie Riordan, the family friend who had supplied the spirit miniatures for Mammy's wake. He was the kind of doctor who would shake a child's hand in greeting, as if you were not a ten-year-old insomniac but a city gent being shown round a country club. Gerry had an outsider's insight into what was plaguing me, and a doctor's knack for saying one thing while doing another. He produced a stethoscope, poked my stomach, felt my pulse and said, as if we had just been speaking on the very subject, 'Tell me, Séamas, what are you so sad about?'

'I don't want Daddy to die,' I replied, in that very moment thinking and saying those words for the first time. This simple act of open thought caused my legs to buckle and I burst into tears. I realised that I hadn't thought to cry in years. It felt as though I was breathing soup. Daddy crossed the room and, before he grabbed me, I could see he had red eyes and a wobbly lip. He placed a massive hand on my head and held me to his chest. All decorum was lost and my sobs grew less reserved. Within seconds I was pushing a microwave lasagne out through my sinus cavities onto his heaving stomach.

'I'm not going anywhere, pet,' he said in a throttled, throat-clearing kind of a voice, with me shaking in his arms. I stayed clamped to him, a baby spider cleaved to his father. I apologised for his ruined tie, and he told me he loved me and basically promised he would never die. It's a promise to which I still hold him.

Dr Gerry waited a respectful minute before informing us that I needed to get to hospital immediately. Whatever the cause of my sadness, my appendix was about to explode.

When the IRA began decommissioning its arms at the end of the nineties, bombings became less frequent altogether. Fay undoubtedly missed the removal of her favourite topic from public discourse, but she told me the real downside was the headaches and heart attacks it was causing local cows. Decommissioning meant rendering the IRA's stores of guns, munitions and explosives inoperable and dumping them in undisclosed sites around the countryside. This was done with independent observers, their locations never revealed. Fay's uncle, she claimed, knew precisely where they'd gone, and he had the dead cattle to prove it.

Uncle Paudie had come to believe his land verged on to one such dump, in which tonnes of nitroglycerine had been deposited and filled in. Workers in chemical plants talk of a condition termed 'bang head': severe, debilitating headaches caused by prolonged exposure to nitroglycerine. This exposure also bestows a tolerance for the substance's other main effect: dilating your veins and regulating blood flow to the heart. The problem, Fay said, was once you built up this tolerance you'd suffer withdrawal if you were ever deprived of it, leading to the 'Sunday heart attacks' that befell chemical engineers who imbibed industrial nitrates at work, only to suffer cardiac arrest once that dependence was interrupted at the weekend.

Uncle Paudie was sure some residue must have seeped into the water table, since his cows all started getting headaches, although the exact manner in which one discerns a cow's headache went unreported. It was only once they were moved indoors that the heart attacks started. A few at first, then more, until he had an entire building filled with bovine corpses and his livestock population had dwindled to those small few who were left, all groaning in various states of cephalalgia.

I didn't stake much on the veracity of Fay's story, since it had the hallmarks of pub-friendly rural myth, and this was the same woman who later told me, five full years after the euro replaced the punt as Irish currency, that she'd never used it, and still bought everything with 'old money'. This was a lie so patently futile I still don't know what she intended to gain by telling it. The truth of Uncle Paudie's cattle was less important than its lessons on unintended consequences. There was a sinister poetry to the notion that burying the poisons of the past led Derry to a future without daily bombings, while also filling a muddy shed in Carrigart with dead and dying cows.

*

They say that the pain of bereavement never leaves you. But it is easier if it's all you've really known. I was so young when Mammy died that I sometimes felt as though I didn't know her well enough to grieve the same way my older siblings did, and that it was somehow false for me to claim the same pain as them. I think I've struggled with the shame of this my entire life. I did not experience the same grief as other members of my family, or friends who've been similarly bereaved, because it happened before I was able to understand it. The funny version of this story is the anecdote that forms the title of this book, but that hides a deeper sense of inadequacy, that my high placing on the hierarchy of grief was false, inauthentic. To a large extent, me telling this story is designed to hide that shame. It's true that my experience simply wasn't the same as that of my older brothers and sisters, and couldn't be. I still sometimes feel embarrassed when grieving friends approach me for advice, as if I could ever review the coping methods used so successfully by that chirpy little five-year-old and write them the same prescription. 'Right, here's my advice – are you taking this down? Step one: be five.'

In truth, the pain didn't leave as well as I thought it had. I muddled through the shallow understanding of grief my five-year-old self could manage, and when the collective tears died down I told myself the job was done. I'd buried it, out of fear and shame and an inability to know how and when to grieve for myself. So, during sleepless nights, it stopped waiting for my permission and sought its own way out. Its price was not waived, but deferred, and the bill had finally arrived. I would have other breakdowns throughout my life, in churches, at roadsides, or standing beneath giant zoologically suspect arachnid sculptures, each born from further layers of unprocessed pain that had accumulated, like heaps of dead munitions, below the surface.

I don't even know that I'd have it any other way. Convincing yourself that tragedy can be avoided may be unhealthy, but it's a lot more enjoyable than the alternative. I never learned to process grief the right way, so maybe it was better to let it do its thing in the background and rely on some more serious part of myself to carry out the intermittent controlled explosions I needed.

My appendix never did explode, in the end. The doctors rushed me into an operating theatre and removed it. As I was being prepped for surgery, I felt calm and resolute, as if the appendix had itself been the pain I was suppressing, and its removal would be the end of my troubles. To some extent this was true, since my insomnia never returned, even if it wasn't my last bout with grief itself.

Daddy wasn't there when I woke up after surgery. It was early in the afternoon, and he was back in the house tearing the place apart to find *The Witches* by Roald Dahl, the one thing I'd mentioned when he asked if I needed anything from home. I awoke to three women sitting next to each other by my bed.

Five years after her death, they had each, independently, heard that I was Sheila's boy. Despite clearly having been at the hospital on other business, they'd stopped by and were effectively queuing to speak with me. To speak with me about Mammy. Even at the time I noted that they must have pulled two chairs from elsewhere, since there had only been one beside my bed when I went under. From their demeanour, I gathered they'd been there a while, and at least one looked as though she'd been roused from sleep around the same time as I had.

'She was a *lady*,' the first of them said as she took my hand. She was blond and tired, and the hand that held mine sported a cannula, bandaged like a primary-school art project. She addressed me not merely as an adult but as though I was the prince of some fallen regent, squeezing my fingers for emphasis as she spoke. 'Your mother was a real lady. God putting people like her on Earth was only spoiling us.' The others agreed, and over the next while they took turns telling me how much she had touched them in their lives, either from her stint in hospital, teaching, Mass groups or other work she did for no reason other than kindness. I said little, and soon they were speaking among themselves, and laughing over this or that thing she'd said or done.

I fell into an easy sleep, scored by their soft, pleasing words. They spoke of my likeness to her, and of my father's strength, and where they'd been when they heard that Mammy died.

Acknowledgements

My agent Matthew Hamilton, for agreeing to meet, and then represent me, at a time when I would likely have accepted a punnet of spuds from any literary type who spelled my name right. And for being the staunch ally and friend I needed in my corner every time it has subsequently been spelled wrong (among other crimes).

Ursula Doyle, who chanced upon a Twitter thread I wrote about meeting Mary McAleese while on ketamine (me that is, not her or Mary) and decided I was the right person to write a heartfelt childhood memoir. Thank you for being a relentless champion of my work, even when I was getting in the way of that work with a disgraceful overuse of adjectives and old-timey references. This book literally would not exist without her, and if it did it would be very, extremely, definitely not good.

Eva Wiseman, who read the same Twitter thread and offered me a parenting column in the *Observer Magazine*. It surely must have seemed an even less likely prospect given the source material, but it has been the joy of my life for the past three years. Thanks to you and to Harriet Green for taking that punt and for being such undying delights to work/chat with since.

Laurence Mackin, who seized on the potential of an incredibly silly Facebook post about fake podcasts to get me my first bylines in the *Irish Times*, and became my first friend and confidant in the chip-paper business. And for forgiving me that time I failed to record an interview with Laurie Anderson, rendering useless the bonhomie I'd established over the course of our hour-long conversation.

Hugh Linehan and Martin Doyle for continuing to publish me on a semi-regular basis, even as I insist on waging a one-man war to make everything about comics.

My *Irish Times* support crew: Jenn, Louise and Peter, who were rocks of support in the absence of water coolers or late-night bars we could loudly mingle around.

Tom Morris, who was the first person who ever grabbed me by the short hairs and got me to actually write something.

Roisin Agnew, of the mighty, much-missed *GUTS* magazine, who was the first person to grab me by the same and receive something publishable.

To my 12 Key Bros, Undesirable Guests, and HFE Cru, you know who you are.

To Mary Agnew, who read the book before anyone else and even confirmed it was borderline readable, and to her, Neave, Manu and Rohan for being the best pals I could ever wish for.

Anne O'Donnell, who was a pillar of strength for my mother during her illness, and for all of us after she died. Your work throughout the period covered in this book helped keep us going, and I've never thanked you enough.

Patricia Donnelly, for being a source of love and laughter across my entire life, and a truly priceless ambassador for my mother's memory since I was old enough to barrage you with questions. (And barrage you I certainly did.) In preserving my mother's letters, you kept more of her alive for us than you could ever imagine. But even that is secondary to the life you breathe into her memory every time you speak of her.

My auntie Aileen McGullion, whose unwavering support and love has been a constant in our lives, not to mention hosting all of us for weeks in the events described in *Jeremy*. Thank you for giving your time to be quizzed by me on everything about that time and about Mammy, and for doing so with such joy that I don't think we stopped laughing for more than a few seconds throughout. I would like to formally apologise for bouncing on the bed as I told you the bad news, but am glad you saw the bleak humour in it too.

My siblings (presented in age order and all in one breath) Sinead, Dara, Shane, Orla, Maeve, Mairead, Dearbhaile, Caoimhe, Fionnuala and Conall. Telling this story meant, to some extent, telling your story but leaving you out of large parts of it. Thank you for tolerating this imposition into your own childhoods, and sorry if you feel I didn't give you enough mentions, or too many mentions by half. Thank you for being kind and patient with me as I peppered you with questions for this book, which I took as a wonderful excuse to find out things about Mammy, yourselves, and myself, that I never would otherwise have asked. The nuggets of family lore that filled our now famous Best Face Forward WhatsApp group is one of the most treasured archives a writer, or a brother, could ever dream of. I love you all.

My father Joe, who features prominently in this book, but even more prominently in my thoughts and feelings every day. To some extent, this entire book is one long thank you to you, and the sacrifices you made to make my childhood one that contained as much humour and absurdity as it did. I don't think even you understand what a gift that's been to me, and to all of us. Thank you for being as generous with your memories – granted, after a certain amount of wheedling from me – as you have been with your time, energy and understanding throughout my life. I can't wait to hear your every objection and correction to each error and misapprehension you find in these pages. Where I have stretched reality to grasp a joke, I hope you'll understand, or offer forgiveness. You have forgiven me for worse in the past. For that and for everything else, I can't ever thank you enough.

I'd like to thank my wonderful wife Ciara for her reassurance, criticism and undying support, not least literal financial support when I quit my job to write full time. A lot of writing is spent thinking you're not very good, so it's occasionally useful to have someone around who's not afraid to put that suspicion outside all doubt. And there's no better feeling than when you – specifically you – like something I've done. My mission in life remains to make you laugh, and I am glad the book has even now had good reason to make you cry once or twice. I adore you beyond words but, since that's what books are made of, they'll have to do this once. I love you.

And to Ruadh, the bright, burning star in my sky, who makes life better, sweeter and happier every single day he's in it. Each extra layer of depth you've added to my heart has helped me dig deeper into the deep stuff. I could not have written this book without you.